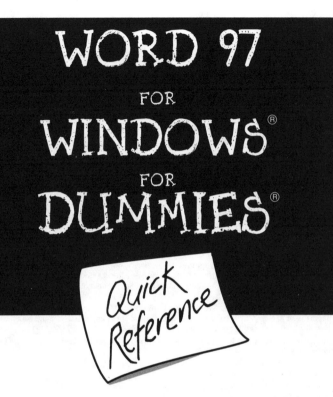

WORD 97
FOR
WINDOWS®
FOR
DUMMIES®
Quick Reference

by Peter Weverka

TM

IDG
BOOKS
WORLDWIDE

IDG Books Worldwide, Inc.
An International Data Group Company

Foster City, CA ✦ Chicago, IL ✦ Indianapolis, IN ✦ Southlake, TX

Word 97 For Windows® For Dummies® Quick Reference

Published by
IDG Books Worldwide, Inc.
An International Data Group Company
919 E. Hillsdale Blvd.
Suite 400
Foster City, CA 94404
www.idgbooks.com (IDG Books Worldwide Web site)
www.dummies.com (Dummies Press Web site)

Library of Congress Catalog Card No.: 96-79265

ISBN: 0-7645-0070-8

Printed in the United States of America

10 9 8 7 6 5 4 3

1P/RZ/RS/ZX/IN

Distributed in the United States by IDG Books Worldwide, Inc.

Distributed by Macmillan Canada for Canada; by Transworld Publishers Limited in the United Kingdom; by IDG Norge Books for Norway; by IDG Sweden Books for Sweden; by Woodslane Pty. Ltd. for Australia; by Woodslane Enterprises Ltd. for New Zealand; by Longman Singapore Publishers Ltd. for Singapore, Malaysia, Thailand, and Indonesia; by Simron Pty. Ltd. for South Africa; by Toppan Company Ltd. for Japan; by Distribuidora Cuspide for Argentina; by Livraria Cultura for Brazil; by Ediciencia S.A. for Ecuador; by Addison-Wesley Publishing Company for Korea; by Ediciones ZETA S.C.R. Ltda. for Peru; by WS Computer Publishing Corporation, Inc., for the Philippines; by Unalis Corporation for Taiwan; by Contemporanea de Ediciones for Venezuela; by Computer Book & Magazine Store for Puerto Rico; by Express Computer Distributors for the Caribbean and West Indies. Authorized Sales Agent: Anthony Rudkin Associates for the Middle East and North Africa.

For general information on IDG Books Worldwide's books in the U.S., please call our Consumer Customer Service department at 800-762-2974. For reseller information, including discounts and premium sales, please call our Reseller Customer Service department at 800-434-3422.

For information on where to purchase IDG Books Worldwide's books outside the U.S., please contact our International Sales department at 415-655-3200 or fax 415-655-3295.

For information on foreign language translations, please contact our Foreign & Subsidiary Rights department at 415-655-3021 or fax 415-655-3281.

For sales inquiries and special prices for bulk quantities, please contact our Sales department at 415-655-3200 or write to the address above.

For information on using IDG Books Worldwide's books in the classroom or for ordering examination copies, please contact our Educational Sales department at 800-434-2086 or fax 817-251-8174.

For press review copies, author interviews, or other publicity information, please contact our Public Relations department at 415-655-3000 or fax 415-655-3299.

For authorization to photocopy items for corporate, personal, or educational use, please contact Copyright Clearance Center, 222 Rosewood Drive, Danvers, MA 01923, or fax 508-750-4470.

About the Author

Peter Weverka is the author of seven computer books, including *Dummies 101: Word 97 For Windows* and *Dummies 101: Microsoft Office 97 For Windows,* both by IDG Books Worldwide, Inc., and *Quicken 6 for Busy People* by Osborne/McGraw-Hill. His humorous articles and stories (none related to computers, thankfully) have appeared in *Harper's* and the *Exquisite Corpse.*

Peter is also an editor. He has polished, cleaned up, and actually read over 80 computer books on topics ranging from word processing to desktop publishing to the Internet. He edited about 50 of those books online with Microsoft Word.

Peter believes that the goal of all computing is to help you get your work done faster so you don't have to sit in front of the computer anymore. His favorite pastime is pruning trees; his greatest pleasure, jawing with his children.

ABOUT IDG BOOKS WORLDWIDE

Welcome to the world of IDG Books Worldwide.

IDG Books Worldwide, Inc., is a subsidiary of International Data Group, the world's largest publisher of computer-related information and the leading global provider of information services on information technology. IDG was founded more than 25 years ago and now employs more than 8,500 people worldwide. IDG publishes more than 275 computer publications in over 75 countries (see listing below). More than 60 million people read one or more IDG publications each month.

Launched in 1990, IDG Books Worldwide is today the #1 publisher of best-selling computer books in the United States. We are proud to have received eight awards from the Computer Press Association in recognition of editorial excellence and three from *Computer Currents'* First Annual Readers' Choice Awards. Our best-selling *...For Dummies®* series has more than 30 million copies in print with translations in 30 languages. IDG Books Worldwide, through a joint venture with IDG's Hi-Tech Beijing, became the first U.S. publisher to publish a computer book in the People's Republic of China. In record time, IDG Books Worldwide has become the first choice for millions of readers around the world who want to learn how to better manage their businesses.

Our mission is simple: Every one of our books is designed to bring extra value and skill-building instructions to the reader. Our books are written by experts who understand and care about our readers. The knowledge base of our editorial staff comes from years of experience in publishing, education, and journalism — experience we use to produce books for the '90s. In short, we care about books, so we attract the best people. We devote special attention to details such as audience, interior design, use of icons, and illustrations. And because we use an efficient process of authoring, editing, and desktop publishing our books electronically, we can spend more time ensuring superior content and spend less time on the technicalities of making books.

You can count on our commitment to deliver high-quality books at competitive prices on topics you want to read about. At IDG Books Worldwide, we continue in the IDG tradition of delivering quality for more than 25 years. You'll find no better book on a subject than one from IDG Books Worldwide.

IDG BOOKS WORLDWIDE

John Kilcullen
CEO
IDG Books Worldwide, Inc.

Steven Berkowitz
President and Publisher
IDG Books Worldwide, Inc.

VIII
WINNER

Eighth Annual
Computer Press
Awards ≥1992

IX
WINNER

Ninth Annual
Computer Press
Awards ≥1993

X
WINNER

Tenth Annual
Computer Press
Awards ≥1994

XI
WINNER

Eleventh Annual
Computer Press
Awards ≥1995

IDG Books Worldwide, Inc., is a subsidiary of International Data Group, the world's largest publisher of computer-related information and the leading global provider of information services on information technology. International Data Group publishes over 275 computer publications in over 75 countries. Sixty million people read one or more International Data Group publications each month. International Data Group's publications include: ARGENTINA: Buyer's Guide, Computerworld Argentina, PC World Argentina; AUSTRALIA: Australian Macworld, Australian PC World, Australian Reseller News, Computerworld, IT Casebook, Network World, Publish, Webmaster; AUSTRIA: Computerwelt Oesterreich, Networks Austria, PC Tip Austria; BANGLADESH: PC World Bangladesh; BELARUS: PC World Belarus; BELGIUM: Data News; BRAZIL: Annuário de Informática, Computerworld, Connections, Macworld, PC Player, PC World, Publish, Reseller News, Supergamepower; BULGARIA: Computerworld Bulgaria, Network World Bulgaria, PC & MacWorld Bulgaria; CANADA: CIO Canada, Client/Server World, ComputerWorld Canada, InfoWorld Canada, NetworkWorld Canada, WebWorld; CHILE: Computerworld Chile, PC World Chile; COLOMBIA: Computerworld Colombia, PC World Colombia; COSTA RICA: PC World Centro America; THE CZECH AND SLOVAK REPUBLICS: Computerworld Czechoslovakia, Macworld Czech Republic, PC World Czechoslovakia; DENMARK: Communications World Danmark, Computerworld Danmark, Macworld Danmark, PC World Danmark, Techworld Denmark; DOMINICAN REPUBLIC: PC World Republica Dominicana; ECUADOR: PC World Ecuador; EGYPT: Computerworld Middle East, PC World Middle East; EL SALVADOR: PC World Centro America; FINLAND: MikroPC, Tietoverkko, Tietoviikko; FRANCE: Distributique, Hebdo, Info PC, Le Monde Informatique, Macworld, Reseaux & Telecoms, WebMaster France; GERMANY: Computer Partner, Computerwoche, Computerwoche Extra, Computerwoche FOCUS, Global Online, Macwelt, PC Welt; GREECE: Amiga Computing, GamePro Greece, Multimedia World; GUATEMALA: PC World Centro America; HONDURAS: PC World Centro America; HONG KONG: Computerworld Hong Kong, PC World Hong Kong, Publish in Asia; HUNGARY: ABCD CD-ROM, Computerworld Szamitastechnika, Internetto online Magazine, PC World Hungary, PC-X Magazin Hungary; ICELAND: Tolvuheimur PC World Island; INDIA: Information Communications World, Information Systems Computerworld, PC World India, Publish in Asia; INDONESIA: InfoKomputer PC World, Komputek Computerworld, Publish in Asia; IRELAND: ComputerScope, PC Live!; ISRAEL: Macworld Israel, People & Computers/Computerworld; ITALY: Computerworld Italia, Macworld Italia, Networking Italia, PC World Italia; JAPAN: DTP World, Macworld Japan, Nikkei Personal Computing, OS/2 World Japan, SunWorld Japan, Windows NT World, Windows World Japan; KENYA: PC World East African; KOREA: Hi-Tech Information, Macworld Korea, PC World Korea, Publish in Asia; MACEDONIA: PC World Macedonia; MALAYSIA: Computerworld Malaysia, PC World Malaysia, Publish in Asia; MALTA: PC World Malta; MEXICO: Computerworld Mexico, PC World Mexico; MYANMAR: PC World Myanmar; NETHERLANDS: Computer! Totaal, LAN Internetworking Magazine, LAN World Buyers Guide, Macworld Netherlands, Net, WebWereld; NEW ZEALAND: Absolute Beginners Guide and Plain & Simple Series, Computer Buyer, Computer Industry Directory, Computerworld New Zealand, MTB, Network World, PC World New Zealand; NICARAGUA: PC World Centro America; NORWAY: Computerworld Norge, CW Rapport, Datamagasinet, Financial Rapport, Kursguide Norge, Macworld Norge, Multimediaworld Norge, PC World Ekspress Norge, PC World Nettverk, PC World Norge, PC World ProduktGuide Norge; PAKISTAN: Computerworld Pakistan; PANAMA: PC World Panama; PEOPLE'S REPUBLIC OF CHINA: China Computer Users, China Computerworld, China InfoWorld, China Telecom World Weekly, Computer & Communication, Electronic Design China, Electronics Today, Electronics Weekly, Game Software, PC World China, Popular Computer Week, Software Weekly, Software World, Telecom World; PERU: Computerworld Peru, PC World Profesional Peru, PC World SoHo Peru; PHILIPPINES: Click!, Computerworld Philippines, PC World Philippines, Publish in Asia; POLAND: Computerworld Poland, Computerworld Special Report Poland, Cyber, Macworld Poland, Networld Poland, PC World Komputer; PORTUGAL: Cerebro/PC World, Computerworld/Correio Informático, Dealer World Portugal, Mac*In/PC*In Portugal, Multimedia World; PUERTO RICO: PC World Puerto Rico; ROMANIA: Computerworld Romania, PC World Romania, Telecom Romania; RUSSIA: Computerworld Russia, Mir PK, Publish, Seti; SINGAPORE: Computerworld Singapore, PC World Singapore, Publish in Asia; SLOVENIA: Monitor; SOUTH AFRICA: Computing SA, Network World SA, Software World SA; SPAIN: Computerworld España, Communicaciones World España, Dealer World España, Macworld España, PC World España; SRI LANKA: Infolink PC World; SWEDEN: CAP&Design, Computer Sweden, Corporate Computing Sweden, Internetworld Sweden, it.branschen, Macworld Sweden, MaxiData Sweden, MikroDatorn, Nätverk & Kommunikation, PC World Sweden, PCaktiv, Windows World Sweden; SWITZERLAND: Computerworld Schweiz, Macworld Schweiz, PCtip; TAIWAN: Computerworld Taiwan, Macworld Taiwan, NEW ViSiON/Publish, PC World Taiwan, Windows World Taiwan; THAILAND: Publish in Asia, Thai Computerworld; TURKEY: Computerworld Turkiye, Macworld Turkiye, Network World Turkiye, PC World Turkiye; UKRAINE: Computerworld Kiev, Multimedia World Ukraine, PC World Ukraine; UNITED KINGDOM: Acorn User UK, Amiga Format UK, Amiga Computing UK, Apple Talk UK, Computing, Macworld, Parents and Computers UK, PC Advisor, PC Home, PSX Pro, The WEB; UNITED STATES: Cable in the Classroom, CIO Magazine, Computerworld, DOS World, Federal Computer Week, GamePro Magazine, InfoWorld, I-Way, Macworld, Network World, PC Games, PC World, Publish, Video Event, THE WEB Magazine, and WebMaster; online webzines: JavaWorld, NetscapeWorld, and SunWorld Online; URUGUAY: InfoWorld Uruguay; VENEZUELA: Computerworld Venezuela, PC World Venezuela; and VIETNAM: PC World Vietnam. 3/24/97

Author's Acknowledgments

This book owes a lot to a lot of different people. I am especially grateful to IDG Books Worldwide Assistant Acquisitions Editor Gareth Hancock and to Diane Steele, who have believed in my writing and have given me many wonderful opportunities to write books for IDG Books, this one included.

I also wish to thank Michael Simsic, who copyedited the manuscript, and Pam Mourouzis, who worked so hard on the last edition. Not every author is as lucky as I am when it comes to getting good copy editors.

Thanks as well go to technical editor Jim McCarter, who did a superb job of making sure that every task in this book is indeed explained correctly, and to Steve Rath, who wrote the index. Bill Helling, the project editor, is a stellar example of grace under pressure, and I am thankful for that.

I also owe a debt to these people at IDG Books who worked so hard on my book: Valery Bourke, Angie Hunckler, and all the Production team.

Finally, my heartfelt thanks go to my family — Sofia, Henry, and Addie — who were most indulgent of my odd working hours and my strange, vampire-like demeanor in the morning.

Dedication

For Ethel and Bob.

Publisher's Acknowledgments

We're proud of this book; please register your comments through our IDG Books World-wide Online Registration Form located at http://my2cents.dummies.com.

Some of the people who helped bring this book to market include the following:

Acquisitions, Development, and Editorial

Project Editor: Bill Helling

Assistant Acquisitions Editor: Gareth Hancock

Media Development Manager: Joyce Pepple

Copy Editor: Michael Simsic

Technical Editor: Jim McCarter

Editorial Manager: Mary C. Corder

Editorial Assistant: Chris H. Collins

Production

Project Coordinator: Valery Bourke

Layout and Graphics: Brett Black, Cameron Booker, Dominique DeFelice, Maridee V. Ennis, Angela F. Hunckler, Todd Klemme, Jane E. Martin, Brent Savage, Kate Snell

Proofreaders: Joel K. Draper, Henry Lazarek, Rachel Garvey, Nancy Price, Robert Springer, Carrie Voorhis

Indexer: Steve Rath

General and Administrative

IDG Books Worldwide, Inc.: John Kilcullen, CEO; Steven Berkowitz, President and Publisher

IDG Books Technology Publishing: Brenda McLaughlin, Senior Vice President and Group Publisher

Dummies Technology Press and Dummies Editorial: Diane Graves Steele, Vice President and Associate Publisher; Mary Bednarek, Acquisitions and Product Development Director; Kristin A. Cocks, Editorial Director

Dummies Trade Press: Kathleen A. Welton, Vice President and Publisher; Kevin Thornton, Acquisitions Manager; Maureen F. Kelly, Editorial Coordinator

IDG Books Production for Dummies Press: Beth Jenkins, Production Director; Cindy L. Phipps, Manager of Project Coordination, Production Proofreading, and Indexing; Kathie S. Schutte, Supervisor of Page Layout; Shelley Lea, Supervisor of Graphics and Design; Debbie J. Gates, Production Systems Specialist; Robert Springer, Supervisor of Proofreading; Debbie Stailey, Special Projects Coordinator; Tony Augsburger, Supervisor of Reprints and Bluelines; Leslie Popplewell, Media Archive Coordinator

Dummies Packaging and Book Design: Patti Crane, Packaging Specialist; Lance Kayser, Packaging Assistant; Kavish + Kavish, Cover Design

◆

The publisher would like to give special thanks to Patrick J. McGovern, without whom this book would not have been possible.

◆

Table of Contents

Part V: Making Your Work Go Faster 99

Part VI: Desktop Publishing 133

How to Use This Book

Keep this book on the corner of your desk. When you want to try something new, want to try something you're unsure of, or tell yourself that *there has to be a better way,* open this book, and I'll tell you what it is and how to do it.

This little book cannot cover every nook and cranny of Microsoft Word 97, but it covers the fundamental things that everybody needs to know. And it gives you enough instruction so that you can get going on the complicated things.

Over the years, I've discovered a lot of shortcuts and tricks for using this program. I've thrown them into the mix, too, so that you can be the beneficiary of my many years of blind groping and daring experimentation.

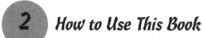

What's in This Book, Anyway?

To find what you're looking for in this book, your best bet is to go to the index and table of contents. Other than that, I've organized this book into eight parts, and you are invited to browse in one part or another until you find what you are looking for.

✦ Part I describes basic techniques and translates ugly word-processing jargon into modern American English.

✦ Part II explains the editing tasks that everyone who wants to use this program wisely should know. You'll find a lot of shortcuts in Part II.

✦ Part III describes formatting. A document communicates by its words but also by the way it is laid out. In Part III, I tell you how to format a document so that readers know exactly what you're about just by glancing at the page.

✦ In Part IV, I explain printing. When you can't print things correctly, it's a nightmare. I hope you never have to visit Part IV.

✦ Part V tells you how to make your work go faster. If you're going to browse, browse in Part V. You'll discover things that you wouldn't think to look for on your own.

✦ Part VI sort of picks up where Part III left off. In many ways, Word 97 is more of a desktop publishing program than a word processing program. Part VI looks at Word's desktop publishing features.

✦ Part VII delves into the fancy and the esoteric. It explains cross-references, footnotes, tables of contents, and other things of use to people who create complex documents.

✦ Part VIII is a hodgepodge conglomeration of the strange and useful. It explains how to back up documents, find missing files, and see how many minutes you've worked on a document, among other things.

✦ At the end of this book is a short glossary of computer terms. If you need to know what "cursor," "field," "cell," and other peculiar terms mean, have a look in the glossary.

The Cast of Icons

To help you get more out of this book, I've placed icons here and there. Here's what the icons mean:

Microsoft Weird 97 has a few odd features and quirks. You can't spell words certain ways without being "AutoCorrected," for example. Try entering a lowercase letter after a period — you can't do it. Word does weird things because it makes a lot of assumptions about what the typical user wants. You, however, may not be a typical user. When I describe the weird things that Word does, I'll put a Weirdness icon in the margin.

Of course, Word 97 has a lot of great stuff too. I'm sure you know that, or else you wouldn't be using Word 97. Where I describe how to use Word's speedy, wonderful, advantageous, effective, and powerful features (I'm getting these adjectives from the Thesaurus), I'll put a Cool Stuff icon in the margin.

Next to the Tip icon, you'll find shortcuts and tricks of the trade.

Where you see this icon, tread softly and carefully. It means that you are opening Pandora's box or doing something you might regret later.

In Word 97, there are usually two ways to do everything — the fast but dicey way and the slow but thorough way. When I explain how to do a task the fast way, I'll put a Fast Track icon in the margin.

If you need more information than this book provides, look for these icons. They tell you which topics are covered in more detail in other *...For Dummies* (IDG Books Worldwide, Inc.) books.

Conventions Used in This Book

To help you learn quickly and get the most out of this book, I've adopted a few conventions.

Where I tell you to click a button, a picture of the button appears in the left-hand margin. For example, the button you see here is the Save button. Where I tell you to "click the Save button to save your document," you'll see the Save button out to the left so that you know exactly which button to click.

Besides clicking buttons, you can do tasks in Word 97 by pressing combinations of keys. For example, you can save a document by pressing Ctrl+S. In other words, you can press the Ctrl key and the S key at the same time. Where you see Ctrl+, Alt+, or Shift+ and a key name (or maybe more than one key name), press the keys simultaneously.

To show how to issue commands, I use the ⇨ symbol. For example, you can choose File⇨Save to save a command. The ⇨ is just a shorthand method of saying, "Choose Save from the File menu."

Notice how the *F* in *File* and the *S* in *Save* are underlined in the preceding paragraph. Those same characters are underlined in the command names in Word 97. Underlined letters are called *hot keys*. You can press them to give commands and make selections in dialog boxes. Where a letter is underlined in a command name or on a dialog box in Word 97, it is also underlined on the pages of this book.

Step-by-step directions in this book are numbered to make directions easier to follow. When you're doing a task, do it by the numbers. Sometimes, however, you have to make choices in order to give a command. When you have to make a choice in a dialog box or you have different options for completing a task, I present the choices in a bulleted list. For example, here are the three ways to save a document:

✦ Choose File⇔Save

✦ Press Ctrl+S

✦ Click the Save button

Where you see letters in boldface text in this book, it means to type the letters. For example, if you read "Type **annual report** in the File Name text box to name your document," you should do just that. You should type those very same letters.

Finally, a word about how option names are capitalized in Word 97 dialog boxes. In the dialog boxes, many option names are shown in lowercase (except for the first letter of the first word). For example, in the Print dialog box you can find an option called Number of copies. In this book, however, that option is called Number of Copies, with a capital *C* for *copies*. I capitalize the first letter to make it easier for you to read option names in this book. Therefore, don't worry if the option names in this book are a little different from the ones in Word 97 dialog boxes.

Smooth Sailing, Reader

Best of luck to you. Every trick I know of for getting the most out of Word 97 is in this book. If you've discovered a trick of your own and would like to share it with me, I would be most grateful. Please e-mail it to me at peter_weverka@msn.com. I'll include it in the next edition of this book and even put your name in lights in the Acknowledgments.

Part 1

Word Processing 101

If you've been around word processors for a while, you needn't read this part of the book. But if you haven't used a word processor before, read on. I'll tell you what mysterious words like *cursor, double-click,* and *scroll* mean. I'll give you the basics so that you can get going with Word 97.

If you aren't yet comfortable with Windows 95, the operating system that Word 97 runs on, you might take a peek at "A Quick Look at Windows 95," the last topic in this part.

In this part . . .

✔ **What a document is, exactly**

✔ **What the cursor and the other weird stuff on-screen are**

✔ **Making menu choices and filling in a dialog box**

✔ **Using the mouse**

✔ **Finding your way around in Windows 95**

What Is a Document?

Document is just a fancy word for a letter, report, announcement, or proclamation that you create with Word 97.

 When you first start Word 97, you see a document with the generic name "Document1." But if you already have a document on-screen and you want to start a new one, click the New button. A brand-new document with the generic name "Document2" in the title bar opens. (The *title bar* is the stripe across the top of the computer screen.) It's called "Document 2" because it's the second one you're working on. The document keeps that name, Document2, until you save it and give it a name of your own.

Say you decide to call your first document "First." When you save it (by clicking the Save button or choosing File⇨Save) and give it the name "First," Word renames it "First."

Cursors, Cursors, and More Cursors

Cursors are little symbols that let you know where you are on-screen or what the computer is doing. There are a bunch of different cursors, but the only ones you really need to know about are listed in the following table:

Cursor	What It Does
I	Sits in the text and blinks on and off. All the action takes place at the insertion point. When you start typing, text appears where the insertion point is. When you paste something from the Clipboard, it appears at the insertion point.

Cursor	What It Does
I ⮖	Moves around on-screen when you move your mouse. Jiggle your mouse to see what the mouse cursor is. When it's over something that you can select — a menu item or a button, for example — it turns into an arrow. Click the mouse when it's an arrow to select a menu item or press a button. When the mouse cursor is over text, it looks like a large, egotistical *I*. To enter text in a new place, move the *I*, click, and start typing.
⌛	When Word 97 is very busy, you see an hourglass on-screen. Twiddle your thumbs until the hourglass disappears and you can get to work.

The Keyboard

Most of the keys on the keyboard are familiar to you, but what about those weird keys camping out on the edges? Start in the upper-left corner of the keyboard and proceed clockwise:

Key (s)	What It Does
Esc	Backs you out of whatever you're doing. If you pull down a menu or dialog box but are frightened by what you see, you can always press Esc to get out.
F1–F12	These are called *function keys.* You press them alone or in combination with the Ctrl and Shift keys to get various things done quickly.
Print Screen, Scroll Lock, Pause	These keys are like the human appendix. They were good for something in the computer's evolutionary past, but now they just take up space on the keyboard.
←	The Backspace key. Press this key to erase letters to the left of the insertion point.
Insert	In most word processing applications, you press this key when you want the letters you type to cover the letters that are already there. Not so in Word 97. Unlike Word 95 and earlier versions of MS Word, pressing the Insert key doesn't allow you to type over existing letters. To do that, double-click OVR on the status bar along the bottom of the screen.
Home	Pressing Home moves the insertion point to the left margin. A second Home key, which does the same thing as the first Home key, appears on the numeric keypad.
Page Up	Press this key to move the insertion point up in the document. It goes up by the length of one computer screen. You'll also find this key on the numeric keypad, along with the number 9, where it has the hiccuppy name PgUp.
Enter	A very important key. Press it to end a paragraph in Word or to say "okay" to the settings in a dialog box.

(continued)

Key (s)	What It Does
Delete	Press this key to remove characters to the right of the insertion point. You can also select sentences, paragraphs, or even whole pages and press Delete to remove gobs of text in one mighty blow. On the numeric keypad, this key is called Del.
End	Moves the insertion point to the end of a line of text. It's also on the numeric keypad.
Page Down	Moves the insertion point downward in a document by the length of one computer screen. This key also appears on the numeric keypad, where you'll find it along with the number 3.
Num Lock	Press Num Lock to make the keys on the numeric keypad act like number keys instead of direction keys. If you're seeing numbers on-screen and you want to move the insertion point instead, Num Lock is on when it shouldn't be. Press Num Lock again to make the keys on the numeric keypad act like direction keys.
← ↑ → and ↓	These *arrow keys,* which share space on the numeric keypad with the 4, 8, 6, and 2, respectively, move the insertion point left, up, right, and down on-screen. You'll find another set of arrow keys at the bottom of the keyboard, between the numeric keypad and the Ctrl key.
Ctrl	The Control key. Press this one along with function keys and letter keys to make Word work quickly. For example, the fastest way to save a document is to press Ctrl+S.
Alt	The Alternate key. Like Ctrl, this is another cattle prod to get Word to do things quickly. Press Alt and one of the underlined letters on the main menu to pull down a menu when you're in a hurry.
Shift	Press this key and a letter to get a capital letter instead of a measly lowercase one.
Caps Lock	Someday soon, you'll be typing along AND DARNIT, YOU'LL START GETTING ALL CAPITAL LETTERS. That's because you accidentally pressed the Caps Lock key. Press it again to go back to lowercase, or just press it if you *want* to type ALL UPPERCASE letters.

Using the Mouse

The *mouse* is the thing you roll across the desk to make the mouse pointer move across your screen. It is called a mouse because the skinny cord that connects it to your computer looks like a mouse's tail. Originally, it was going to be called the *rat,* but someone got squeamish.

The mouse has two buttons. You usually click the left button, although clicking the right button has advantages, too. Try clicking the right button on a part of the screen you're curious about, for example. You'll sometimes see a *shortcut menu* — a list of menu options that pertain to the part of the screen you clicked.

Often, you are asked to *click* the mouse on menu items, icons, and text. When you're asked to click the mouse, click the left mouse button. Only click the right button if you are specifically told to.

You'll do a lot of clicking around in Word. The following table gives you the lowdown on *click* terminology:

Click	What It Means or Does
click	Press the left mouse button quickly.
right-click	Press the right mouse button quickly.
Shift+click	Click the left mouse button while holding down the Shift key.
Ctrl+click	Click the left mouse button while holding down the Control key.
double-click	Press the left mouse button twice — and do it quickly, as though your life depends on it.
click and drag	Press the mouse button and, while still holding it down, drag the mouse over some text. *Dragging* the mouse just means to roll it across your screen. Clicking and dragging is the fastest way to select text.

Making Menu Choices

To do things in Word, you click a button, press a shortcut key combination, or choose an option from a menu.

At the top of the screen is a list of menus called the *main menu:*

File   Edit   View   Insert   Format   Tools   Table   Window   Help

To *pull down* a menu from this list, you can either click the menu name with the mouse or press the Alt key and the letter that is underlined in the menu name. For example, to pull down the File menu, you can either click the word *File* or press Alt+F. When you do, a *pull-down menu* appears as if by magic:

Now you have several *menu commands* to choose from. To choose a command from a pull-down menu, either click the command name or press the letter that is underlined in the command name. Suppose you want to choose the Open command in the File menu. After the File menu drops down, you can either click the word *Open* or press the letter *O* on your keyboard to open a new document.

Shortcut keys for doing it quickly

Notice that some commands on the File menu have Ctrl+key combinations next to their names. These are called *shortcut keys*. If you want to open a document, for example, you can just press Ctrl+O, the shortcut key for opening a document.

Lots of menu commands have shortcut keys that help you get your work done faster. If you find yourself using a command often, see if it has a shortcut key and start using the shortcut key to save time. Many commands have buttons next to their names as well. Instead of choosing these commands from menus, you can simply click a button on a toolbar.

You may also notice that some menu commands have ellipses (three dots) next to their names. When you choose one of these menu commands, a dialog box appears on-screen. *See* "Filling In a Dialog Box" a bit further ahead if you need to know about dialog boxes.

Some commands also have arrows next to their names. Click one of these commands and you get a *submenu* — a short menu with more commands to choose from.

Those mysterious shortcut menus

Shortcut menus are mysterious little menus that sometimes pop up when you click the right mouse button. For example, you get this shortcut menu when you click the right mouse button in the middle of a document:

> ✂ Cu&t
> 📋 &Copy
> 📋 &Paste
>
> A &Font...
> ☰¶ &Paragraph...
> ☰ Bullets and &Numbering...
>
> ✏ Draw Ta&ble
>
> &Define

These are basic editing commands for working on a document.

When you right-click a word with a squiggly red line underneath it, you see a shortcut menu with suggestions for correcting a misspelled word:

> squiggley
>
> **squiggly**
> **squiggle**
> **squiggled**
> **squiggles**
>
> &Ignore All
> A&dd
>
> AutoCorrect ▶
> ✓ &Spelling...

Filling In a Dialog Box

When Word needs a lot of information to complete a command, a *dialog box* appears on-screen. You have to fill out the dialog box before Word will do what you ask it to do. Here's the dialog box you get when you ask Word to print a document, for example:

Radio buttons   Drop-down list   Check boxes   Scroll list

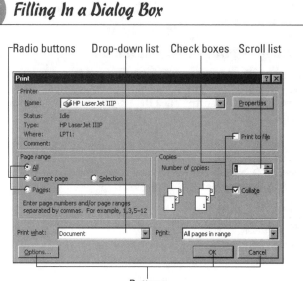

Buttons

At the bottom is a *drop-down list.* Click the arrow that points down, and down comes a list of things such as comments and document properties that you can print in addition to the document itself.

Notice the Number of Copies *scroll list* in the Print dialog box. Click the little arrow that points up, and the number climbs so that you can print two, three, four, or more copies. Click the little down-pointing arrow to get back to four, three, two, and one copy.

Four *radio buttons* tell Word which part of the document to print. The thing to know about radio buttons is that you can only choose one, just like you can listen to only "Super Country KCOW" or "Rockin' KROQ" but not both radio stations at once. In this dialog box, you can print the whole document, the page the cursor is in, a selection of text, or a range of pages.

At the bottom of the Print dialog box are some buttons. Most dialog boxes have an OK and a Cancel button. Click OK (or press Enter) after you've filled out the dialog box and you're ready for Word to execute the command. Click Cancel if you lose your nerve and want to start all over again.

Notice the two *check boxes* in the Print dialog box. You could click both or neither check box. Check boxes work like radio buttons, except that you can select more than one or none at all.

Some dialog boxes have tabs. A *tab* is a thing you click to get another page of settings. For example, the Options dialog box has a grand total of 10 tabs. If you want to change how Word saves documents, click the Save tab. To change the view settings, click the View tab. (Choose Tools⇨Options to see the Options dialog box.)

What All That Stuff On-Screen Is

Seeing the Word 97 screen for the first time is sort of like trying to find your way through Tokyo's busy Ikebukuro subway station. It's intimidating. But once you start using Word 97, you'll quickly learn what everything is. In the meantime, the following table gives you some shorthand descriptions.

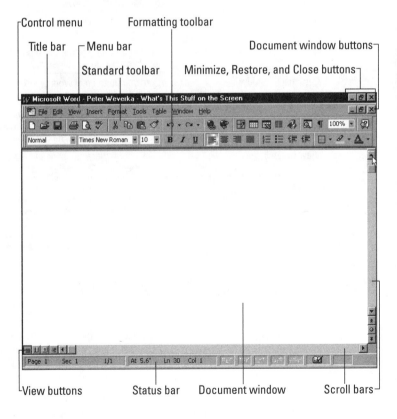

Part of Screen	What It Is
Title bar	At the top of the screen, the title bar tells you the name of the document you're working on and the name of the person who's working on it.
Control menu	Click here to pull down a menu with options for minimizing, maximizing, moving, and closing the window.
Minimize, Restore, Close buttons	These three magic buttons make it very easy to shrink, enlarge, and close the window.
Menu bar	The list of main menu options, from File to Help, that you can choose from to give Word 97 commands.
Document window buttons	Click these buttons to shrink, enlarge, or close the document window.
Standard toolbar	Offers buttons that you can click to execute Word 97 commands.
Formatting toolbar	Offers formatting buttons and pull-down lists for changing the appearance of text.
Document window	Here you do the real work of writing words and laying out text.
Scroll bars	The scroll bars help you move around in a document. See "Moving Around in Documents" in Part II to learn how to use them.
View buttons	Click one of these to change your view of a document.
Status bar	Here's where you can get basic information about where you are and what you're doing in a document. The status bar tells you what page and what section you're in, the total number of pages in the document, where the insertion point is on the page, and the time.

Understanding How Paragraphs Work

Back in English class, your teacher taught you that a paragraph is a part of a longer composition that presents one idea or, in the case of dialogue, presents the words of one speaker. Your teacher was right, too, but for word processing purposes, a paragraph is a lot less than that. In word processing, a paragraph is simply what you put on-screen before you press the Enter key.

For instance, a heading is a paragraph. So is a graphic. If you press Enter on a blank line to go to the next line, the blank line is considered a paragraph. If you type *Dear John* at the top of a letter and press Enter, "Dear John" is a paragraph.

¶ It's important to know this because paragraphs have a lot to do with formatting. If you choose the Format⇨Paragraph command and monkey around with the paragraph formatting, all your changes affect everything in the paragraph that contains the cursor. To make format changes to a whole paragraph, all you have to do is place the cursor there. You don't have to select the paragraph.

Starting Word 97

To start Word 97, all you have to do is this:

1. Click the Start button on the taskbar.

2. Choose Programs.

3. Choose Microsoft Word.

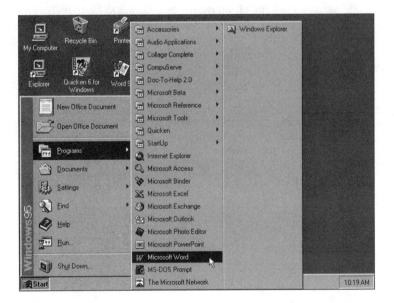

By the way, if all that clicking to start Word strains your wrist, you should know that you can put a shortcut icon on the desktop next to the My Computer and Recycle Bin icons and start Word merely by double-clicking its icon. Or you can set things up so that Word starts whenever you turn on your computer. Get a good book like Andy Rathbone's *Windows 95 For Dummies* (IDG Books Worldwide, Inc.) to find out how.

A Quick Look at Windows 95

Windows 95 is a Microsoft's monolithic operating system. It has
everything in it *including* the kitchen sink, so a little book like this
can't possibly do it justice. Here, I'll just give you the basics. To get all
the dope on Windows 95, read *Windows 95 For Dummies*.

Changing the size of the Word 97 window

By clicking the three buttons on the right side of the title bar, you can
minimize, maximize, shrink, or restore the Word 97 program window:

♦ The Minimize button makes Word 97 disappear from the screen.
But the program is still running. To see the Word screen again
after you click the Minimize button, click Microsoft Word on the
taskbar.

♦ Click the Maximize/Restore button to make the Word window
smaller. When you shrink the screen, the button changes into a
square. Click the square "Restore" button again to make Word 97
window fill the screen.

Switching applications with the taskbar

Along the bottom of the screen is a thing called the *taskbar,* which
allows you to run a bunch of applications all at the same time. The
names of all the applications that are running appear on buttons on
the taskbar. To switch to a new application, click its button. You can
also press Alt+Tab to see the applications that are running one at
a time.

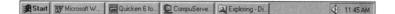

Editing and Other Essentials

In Part II, you'll find instructions for editing and doing the tasks that take up most of your word processing time. Among other things, Part II explains how to create, open, and close files. It tells you how to move around in documents, cut and copy text, and hyphenate and fix spelling errors.

My Word, there are a lot of good things in Part II.

In this part . . .

- ✓ Deleting, selecting, cutting, copying, and pasting text
- ✓ Finding and correcting spelling errors
- ✓ Opening and closing a document
- ✓ Exiting Word 97
- ✓ Saving a document
- ✓ Working with headers, footers, and page numbers
- ✓ Working with more than one document at once
- ✓ Zooming in and out on a document

Breaking a Line

You can break a line in the middle, before it reaches the right margin, without starting a new paragraph. To do that, press Shift+Enter.

By pressing Shift+Enter, you can fix problems in the way Word breaks lines. When words are squeezed into narrow columns, it often pays to break lines to remove ugly white spaces.

This figure shows two identical paragraphs. To make the lines break better, I pressed Shift+Enter before the word *in* in the first line of the paragraph on the right. I did it again in the second-to-last line before the word *annual*. As you can see, the paragraph on the right fits in the column better and is easier to read.

"A computer in every home and a chicken in every pot is our goal," stated Rupert T. Verguenza, President and CEO of the New Technics Corporation International at the annual shareholder meeting this week.	"A computer in every home and a chicken in every pot is our goal," stated Rupert T. Verguenza, President and CEO of the New Technics Corporation International at the annual shareholder meeting this week.

Line breaks are marked with the ↵ symbol. To erase line breaks, click the Show/Hide ¶ button to see these symbols and backspace over them.

Breaking a Page

Word gives you another page so that you can keep going when you fill up one page. But what if you're impatient and want to start a new page right away? Whatever you do, *don't* press Enter over and over until you fill up the page. Instead, create a page break by doing either of the following:

✦ Press Ctrl+Enter.

✦ Choose Insert➪Break, click Page Break, and click OK.

To delete a page break, either delete it or backspace over it. In Normal View, you know when you've inserted a page break yourself because you see the words Page Break and a dotted line instead of the dotted line at the end of the page.

Changing the Look of the Screen

The Word 97 window is cluttered, to say the least, but you can do something about that with options on the View menu:

✦ Choose View⇨Toolbars to remove toolbars. In the submenu, check marks appear beside the toolbars that are on-screen. Click a toolbar's name to remove the check mark and remove it from the screen as well. You can also remove toolbars by right-clicking on a toolbar and clicking the name of the toolbar you want to remove on the shortcut menu.

✦ Choose View⇨Ruler to get rid of the ruler.

✦ Choose View⇨Full Screen if you want to get rid of everything except the text you're working on. When you choose Full Screen, everything gets stripped away — buttons, menus, scroll bars, and all. Only a single button called Close Full Screen remains. Click it or press Esc when you want the buttons, menus, and so on, back. As the following figure shows, you can choose commands from the main menu in Full Screen View by moving the pointer to the top of the screen to make the menu appear. Of course, you can also press shortcut key combinations and right-click to see shortcut menus.

Click to get Word 97 back.

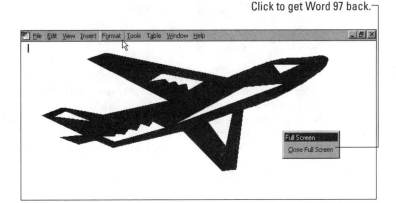

Changing lowercase to UPPERCASE, UPPERCASE to lowercase

What do you do if you look at your screen and discover to your dismay that you entered characters IN THE WRONG CASE! It happens. And sometimes Word does mysterious things to letters at the start of sentences and capital letters in the middle of words. What can you do about that?

You can fix uppercase and lowercase problems in two ways.

The fastest way is to select the text you entered incorrectly and press Shift+F3. Keep pressing Shift+F3 until the text looks right. Shift+F3 changes the characters to all lowercase, then to Initial Capitals, and then to ALL UPPERCASE.

The other way is to select the text, choose Format⇨Change Case, and click an option in the Change Case dialog box:

◆ **Sentence case:** Makes the text look like this.

◆ **lowercase:** makes the text look like this.

◆ **UPPERCASE:** MAKES THE TEXT LOOK LIKE THIS.

◆ **Title Case:** Makes The Text Look Like This.

◆ **tOGGLE cASE:** mAKES THE TEXT LOOK LIKE THIS, AND i WOULD CHOOSE THIS OPTION IF i ACCIDENTALLY TYPED LOTS OF TEXT WITH CAPS LOCK ON.

Change Case	? ☒
○ Sentence case.	OK
○ lowercase	Cancel
◉ UPPERCASE	
○ Title Case	
○ tOGGLE cASE	

Microsoft Weird is very presumptuous about how it thinks capital letters should be used. You've probably noticed that already. You can't type a lowercase letter after a period. You can't enter a new-fangled company name like QUestData because Word refuses to let two capital letters in a row stand. You can't enter lowercase computer code at the start of a line without Word capitalizing the first letter. *See* "Correcting Typos on the Fly" in Part V if you want to change how Word 97 deals with capital letters.

Closing a Document

Choose File⇨Close to close a document when you're done working on it. If you try to close a document and you've made changes to it that you haven't saved yet, you see this dialog box:

Microsoft Word	☒
⚠ Do you want to save the changes you made to Closure?	
Yes	No	Cancel

Click <u>Y</u>es, unless you're abandoning the document because you want to start all over. In that case, click <u>N</u>o.

 Click Word 97's Close button (the *X*) in the upper-right corner of the screen to close a document and shut down Word 97 at the same time.

Copying, Moving, and Pasting Text

Word offers a number of different ways to copy and move text from one place to another. By one place to another, I mean from one part of a document to another, from one document to another document, and from one program to another program. Yes, you can even move and copy data between Windows-based programs.

Here's the conventional way to move or copy text:

1. Select the text to move or copy.

2. Do one of the following:

 • **To move:** Choose <u>E</u>dit⇨<u>Cu</u>t, click the Cut button, or press Ctrl+X.

• **To copy:** Choose <u>E</u>dit⇨<u>C</u>opy, click the Copy button, or press Ctrl + X.

3. Place the cursor where you want to move or copy the text.

4. Choose <u>E</u>dit⇨<u>P</u>aste, click the Paste button, or press Ctrl+V.

When you copy or cut text, it is placed in an electronic holding tank in your computer called the *Clipboard.* It stays there until you cut or copy something new and the new text takes the place of the old text. The Clipboard can only hold one item at a time.

You can paste what is on the Clipboard into a document as many times as you want. If you like to decorate your correspondence with smiling faces, you can copy a smiley face image to the Clipboard and keep pasting it in 'til the cows come home.

 A fast way to cut, copy, and paste is to select the text, right-click it, and choose <u>C</u>ut or <u>C</u>opy from the shortcut menu. Then move the cursor where you want to paste the text, right-click, and choose <u>P</u>aste.

Choose Cut or Copy, then Paste

- ✂ Cu<u>t</u>
- ▣ <u>C</u>opy
- ▣ <u>P</u>aste

- ⬅ <u>D</u>ecrease Indent
- ➡ <u>I</u>ncrease Indent

- A <u>F</u>ont...
- ☰ <u>P</u>aragraph...
- ☰ Bullets and <u>N</u>umbering...

A second, slightly speedier way to move or copy text is to use the drag-and-drop method:

1. Select the text you want to copy or move.

2. Slide the mouse over the selected text until the cursor changes into an arrow.

3. Copy or move the text:

- **To move:** Drag the text to a new location.

- **To copy:** Hold down the Ctrl key while you drag the text elsewhere.

4. Let up on the mouse button.

One neat thing about dragging and dropping is that you can copy or move text without disturbing what's on the Clipboard. Text isn't copied to the Clipboard when you drag and drop.

Dashes

Amateurs make the hyphen do the work of the em dash and en dash. An *em dash* looks like a hyphen but is wider — it's as wide as the letter M. The last sentence has an em dash in it. Did you notice?

An *en dash* is the width of the letter N. En dashes are used to show inclusive numbers or time periods, like so: pp. 45–50, Aug.–Sept. 1996, Exodus 16:11–16:18. An en dash is a little bit longer than a hyphen.

To place em or en dashes in your documents and impress your local typesetter or editor, not to mention your readers:

1. Choose Insert⇨Symbol.

2. Click the Special Characters tab in the Symbol dialog box.

3. Choose Em Dash or En Dash.

4. Click Insert.

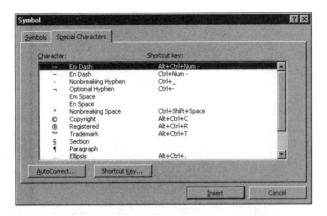

  Another way to create an em dash is by typing two hyphens in a row. Word 97 will turn them into a single em dash.

Deleting Text

To delete a bunch of text at once, select the text you want to delete and press Delete or choose Edit⇨Clear.

 See also "Undoing a Mistake" later in Part II if you delete text and realize to your horror and dismay that you shouldn't have done that.

Deleting a Word Document

When you're finished with a document and you want to delete it, follow these steps:

1. Choose File⇨Open as if you were opening a document, not deleting one.

2. In the Open dialog box, find and right-click the file you want to delete.

3. From the shortcut menu, choose Delete.

4. When Word asks if you really want to go through with it and send the file to the Recycle Bin, click Yes.

5. Click Cancel to remove the Open dialog box.

If you regret deleting a file, you can resuscitate it. Minimize Word and, on the Windows desktop, double-click Recycle Bin. The Recycle Bin opens with a list of the files you deleted. Click the one you regret deleting and choose File⇨Restore in the Recycle Bin.

Exiting Word 97

When it's time to say good-bye to Word 97, save and close all your documents. Then do one of the following:

+ Choose File⇨Exit.

 + Click the Close button (the *X*) on the right side of the title bar.

+ Press Alt+F4.

If perchance you forgot to save and close a document, you'll see the Do you want to save changes? dialog box. Click Yes.

Microsoft Word

Do you want to save the changes you made to Depart?

Yes   No   Cancel

Finding and Replacing Text and Formats

The Edit⇨Replace command is a very powerful one indeed. If you were writing a Russian novel and you decided on page 816 to change the main character's last name from Oblonsky to Oblomov, you could do it on all 816 pages with the Edit⇨Replace command in about a half a minute.

But here's the drawback: You never quite know what this command will do. Newspaper editors tell a story about a newspaper that made it a policy to use the word *African-American* instead of *black*. That is laudable, except a sleepy editor made the change with the Edit⇨Replace command and didn't review it. Next day, a lead story on the business page read, "After years of running in the red, US Steel has paid all its debts, and now the corporation is running well in the African-American, according to company officials."

To replace words, phrases, or formats:

1. Choose Edit⇨Replace or press Ctrl+H.

2. Fill in the Find What box just as you would if you were searching for text or formats (see the "Finding Text and More" entry later in this part to find out how).

3. In the Replace With box, enter the text that will replace what is in the Find What box. If you're replacing a format, enter the format.

4. Either replace everything at once or do it one at a time:

- Click Replace All to make all replacements in an instant.

- Click Find Next and then either click Replace to make the replacement or click Find Next to bypass it.

Word tells you when you're finished.

The sleepy newspaper editor I told you about clicked the Replace All button. Only do that if you're very confident and know exactly what you're doing. In fact, one way to keep from making embarrassing replacements is to start by using the Edit⇨Find command. When you land on the first instance of the thing you are searching for, click the Replace tab and tell Word 97 what should replace the thing you found. This way, you can rest assured that you entered the right search criteria and that Word is finding exactly what you want it to find.

The Edit⊅Replace command is very powerful. *Always* save your document before you use this command. Then, if you replace text that you shouldn't have replaced, you can close your document without saving it, open your document again, and get your original document back.

Finding the Right Word with the Thesaurus

If you can't seem to find the right word, you can always give the Thesaurus a shot. To find synonyms (words that have the same or a similar meaning) for a word in your document:

1. Place the cursor in the word.

2. Choose Tools⊅Language⊅Thesaurus or press Shift+F7.

3. Begin your quest for the right word.

4. When you've found it and it appears in the Replace with Synonym box, click Replace.

Thesaurus: English (British)	? X
Looked Up:	Replace with Synonym:
compact ▼	concise
Meanings:	concise
dense (adj.)	succinct
concise (adj.)	brief
arrangement (noun)	terse
convention (noun)	summary
pack together (verb)	laconic
cement (verb)	pithy
	pointed
Replace	Look Up	Previous	Cancel

Finding the right words is nine-tenths of writing, so the Thesaurus dialog box tries to make it easier by offering these amenities:

✦ **Looked Up:** A drop-down list with all the words you've investigated in your quest. Click a word here to go back to one you've examined (or click the Previous button).

✦ **Meanings:** Different ways the term can be used — as a verb or noun, for example. Click here to turn your search in a different direction. Sometimes there's even an Antonym selection. At worst, if you know the opposite of the word you want, you can look it up in the Thesaurus and find its antonym. You can also try choosing Related Words if you're desperate.

✦ **Replace with Synonym:** If the Thesaurus isn't being helpful, you can always type a word into this box and click the Look Up button.

✦ **Look Up:** Highlight a word in the Replace with Synonym box scroll list and click the Look Up button to investigate that word.

Finding Text and More

You can search for a word in a document, and even for fonts, special characters, and formats. Here's how:

1. Choose Edit⇨Find, press Ctrl+F, or click the Select Browse Object button in the lower-right corner of the screen and choose Find. The Find and Replace dialog box appears.

2. Enter the word, phrase, or format you are looking for in the Find What box (how to enter formats is explained below). Words and phrases you looked for recently are on the Find What drop-down list. Click the down arrow to view and make a selection from the list if you want to.

3. Click the Find Next button if you are looking for a simple word or phrase. Otherwise, click the More button to conduct a sophisticated search before you click Find Next.

If the thing you're looking for can be found, Word highlights it in the document. To find the next instance of the thing you are looking for, click Find Next again, or else close the dialog box and click the Previous Find/Go To or Next Find/Go To button at the bottom of the scroll bar to the right of the screen (or press Ctrl+Page Up or Ctrl+Page Down).

By clicking the More button in the Find and Replace dialog box, you can get very selective about what to search for and how to search for it:

✦ **Search:** Click the down arrow and choose All, Up, or Down to search the whole document, search from the cursor position upward, or search from the cursor position downward.

✦ **Match Case:** Searches for words with upper- and lowercase letters that exactly match those in the Find What box. With this box selected, a search for *bow* finds that word, but not *Bow* or *BOW*.

✦ **Find Whole Words Only:** Normally, a search for *bow* yields *elbow, bowler, bow-wow,* and all other words with the letters *bow* in them. Click this option and you only get *bow*.

✦ **Use Wildcards:** Click here if you intend to use wildcards in searches. *See* "Searching with Wildcards" in Part V if you need instructions for searching this way.

✦ **Sounds Like:** Looks for words that sound like the one in the Find What box. A search for *bow* with this option selected finds *beau,* for example.

✦ **Find All Word Forms:** Takes into account verb endings and plurals. With this option clicked, you get *bows, bowing,* and *bowed,* as well as *bow*.

To search for words, paragraphs, tab settings, and styles, among other things, that are formatted a certain way, click the Format button and choose an option from the menu. You see the familiar dialog box you used in the first place to format the text. In the Find dialog box shown in this book, I choose Font from the Format menu and filled in the Font dialog box in order to search for the word "bow" in Times Roman, 12-point, italicized font.

Click the Special button to look for format characters, manual page breaks, and other unusual stuff.

That No Formatting button is there so that you can clear all the formatting from the Find What box. Once you've found something, you can give Word 97 instructions for replacing it by clicking the Replace tab. To find out about that, you have to read "Finding and Replacing Text and Formats," also in this part.

After you click the More button to get at the sophisticated search options, the button changes its name to Less. In this instance, More is Less. Click the Less button to shrink the dialog box and get more room to work on-screen.

Getting the Help You Need

Word 97 offers a bunch of different ways to get help, and one or two of them are useful. The best way to get help is to choose Help➪Contents and Index. That takes you to a dialog box with three tabs for finding the instructions you need:

✦ **Contents:** A bunch of general topics. Double-click a book icon, and it opens to more topics, each with a question mark beside its name. Click the question mark beside the topic that interests you and click Display, if general topics are your cup of tea.

✦ **Index:** This is the most useful means of getting help. Click the Index tab and type a few letters that describe what puzzles you. The alphabetical list of index topics scrolls down to show you which topics are available. If a topic strikes your fancy, double-click it or click it and choose Display. You'll go straight to an informative instruction box or some other help feature.

✦ **Find:** With this option, you search for a word in the Help files. For example, if you need help with entering accented characters, type **accent.** A list of topics appears at the bottom of the dialog box. Click the topic you're interested in and click Display.

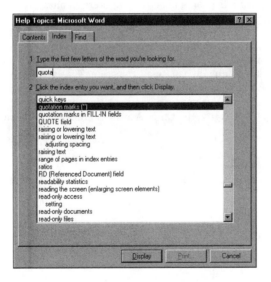

Another useful way to get help is to choose Help⟳What's This or press Shift+F1. The pointer changes into an arrow with a question mark beside it. Click this quizzical cursor on a part of the screen that you want to know more about. With any luck, you get concise instructions for carrying out the thing you clicked. Here is the mini-Help screen you get when you click text to see how it is formatted:

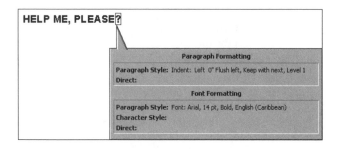

HELP ME, PLEASE❓

Paragraph Formatting
Paragraph Style: Indent: Left 0" Flush left, Keep with next, Level 1
Direct:
Font Formatting
Paragraph Style: Font: Arial, 14 pt, Bold, English (Caribbean)
Character Style:
Direct:

The upper-right corner of dialog boxes also have Help buttons in the shape of question marks. Click on a dialog box Help button and click on the part of the dialog box you need help with to get a brief explanation of the thing you clicked.

In keeping with its goal of making computers as much fun to use as watching Saturday morning cartoons, Microsoft also offers the Office Assistant. Click the Office Assistant button on the Standard toolbar (or press F1) and the Office Assistant — an animated figure — appears in the lower-right corner of the screen along with a bubble caption into which you can type a question. Type your question, click Search, and hope in vain for a sensible answer. After the first and last time you've tried this means of getting help, click the Close button (the *X*) in the box that the Office Assistant comes in to make the little pest dissolve.

The Help menu also has a special command for people who have switched over from the WordPerfect word-processing application and several commands for getting help with using Word 97 on the Internet. To take advantage of the Internet Help commands, you must have signed on with The Microsoft Network.

That last command on the Help menu, About Microsoft Word, is only of interest if your computer dies and you need technical help from Microsoft. I hope that doesn't happen, but if it does, choose this

command and click the <u>T</u>ech Support button to find out how to
contact Microsoft. Hmmm. I just realized something. You couldn't
choose that command if your computer died, could you?

Hyphenating a Document

The first thing you should know about hyphenating a document is
that you may not need to do it. Text that hasn't been hyphenated is
much easier to read — which is why the text in this book isn't hyphenated. It has a *ragged right margin,* to use typesetter lingo. Only hyphenate
when text is trapped in columns or in other narrow places, when it is
justified, or when you want a very formal-looking document.

You can hyphenate text as you enter it, but I think you should wait
until you've written everything so that you can concentrate on the
words themselves. Then when you're done with the writing, you can
either have Word hyphenate the document automatically or you can
do it yourself.

Hyphenating a document automatically

To hyphenate a document automatically:

1. Choose <u>T</u>ools⇨Language⇨Hyphenation.

2. Click <u>A</u>utomatically Hyphenate Document to let Word do the job.

3. Click Hyphenate Words in <u>C</u>APS to remove the check mark.
Never, ever hyphenate uppercase words if you can help it.

4. If the text isn't justified — that is, if it's "ragged right" — you may
play with the Hyphenation <u>Z</u>one setting (but I don't think you
should hyphenate ragged right text anyway). Words that fall in
the Zone are hyphenated, so a large zone means a less ragged
margin but more ugly hyphens, and a small zone means fewer
ugly hyphens but a more ragged right margin.

5. More than two consecutive hyphens in a row on the right margin
looks bad, so enter **2** in the <u>L</u>imit Consecutive Hyphens To box.

6. Click OK.

Hyphenating a document manually

The other way to hyphenate is to see where Word 97 wants to put hyphens and "Yea" or "Nay" them one at a time:

1. Select the part of the document you want to hyphenate, or else place the cursor where you want hyphens to start appearing.

2. Choose Tools⇨Language⇨Hyphenation.

3. Click the Manual button. Word displays a box with some hyphenation choices in it. The cursor blinks on the spot where Word suggests putting a hyphen.

Manual Hyphenation: English (United States)	? ✕
Hyphenate at: `hy-phen-at-ing`	
Yes No Cancel	

4. Click Yes or No to accept or reject Word's suggestion.

5. Keep accepting or rejecting Word's suggestions. At some point, a box appears to tell you that Word has finished hyphenating. To quit hyphenating yourself, click the Cancel button in the Manual Hyphenation dialog box.

A fast way to insert a manual hyphen is to put the cursor where you want the hyphen to go and press Ctrl+hyphen. Press Ctrl+hyphen when there is a big gap in the right margin and a word is crying out to be hyphenated. In this illustration, I pressed Ctrl+hyphen after "antidisestablishmen" in the paragraph on the right to make the line break in a better position.

On a "ragged right" margin, how do you fix the gaps that appear when you use long words like "antidiestablishmentarisnism?" You press Ctrl+hyphen, that's how.	On a "ragged right" margin, how do you fix the gaps that appear when you use long words like "antidiestablishmen-tarisnism?" You press Ctrl+hyphen, that's how.

Unhyphenating and other hyphenation tasks

Here is some more hyphenation esoterica:

✦ To "unhyphenate" a document you hyphenated automatically, choose Tools⇨Language⇨Hyphenation, remove the check from the Automatically hyphenate document box, and click OK. To remove manual hyphens, delete or backspace over them.

✦ To keep a paragraph from being hyphenated, choose Format⇨Paragraph, click the Line and Page Breaks tab, and put a check mark in the Don't hyphenate box. If you can't hyphenate a paragraph, it is probably because this box was checked unintentionally.

✦ If you want to hyphenate a single paragraph in the middle of a document — maybe because it's a long quotation or some other thing that needs to stand out — select it and hyphenate it manually by clicking the Manual button in the Hyphenation dialog box.

Inserting a Whole File in a Document

One of the beautiful things about word processing is that you can recycle documents. Say you wrote an essay on the Scissor-Tailed Flycatcher that would fit very nicely in a broader report on North American birds. You can insert the Scissor-Tailed Flycatcher document in your report document:

1. Place the cursor where you want to insert the document.

2. Choose Insert⇨File.

3. In the Insert File dialog box, find and click on the file you want to insert.

4. Click OK.

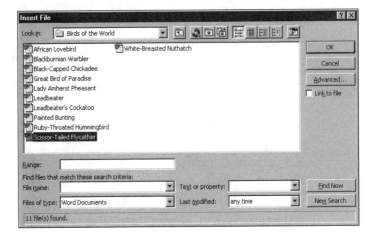

Moving Around in Documents

Documents have a habit of getting longer and longer, and as they do that, it takes more effort to move around in them. Here are some shortcuts for getting here and there in documents.

Keys for getting around quickly

One of the fastest ways to go from place to place is to press keys and key combinations:

Key to Press	Where It Takes You
PgUp	Up the length of one screen
PgDn	Down the length of one screen
Ctrl+PgUp	To the top of the screen
Ctrl+PgDn	To the bottom of the screen
Ctrl+Home	To the top of the document
Ctrl+End	To the bottom of the document

> **TIP**
>
> If pressing Ctrl+PgUp or Ctrl+PgDn doesn't get you to the top or bottom of a page, that's because you clicked the Select Browse Object button at the bottom of the vertical scroll bar, so Word goes to the next bookmark, comment, heading, or whatever. Click the Select Browse Object button and choose Browse by Page to make these key combinations work again.

Zipping around with the scroll bar

You can also use the scroll bar to get around in documents. The *scroll bar* is the vertical stripe along the right side of the screen that resembles an elevator shaft. Here's how to move around with the scroll bar:

✦ To move through a document quickly, grab the elevator (called the *scroll box*) and drag it up or down. As you scroll, a yellow box appears with the page number you are on and the name of the headings on the page you are on (provided you assigned Word styles to those headings).

✦ To move line by line up or down, click the up or down arrow at the top or bottom of the scroll bar.

✦ To move screen by screen, click anywhere on the scroll bar except on the arrows or the elevator.

By the way, there's another scroll bar on the bottom of the screen for moving from side to side.

See also "Going Here, Going There in Documents" and "Bookmarks for Hopping Around" in Part V for more moving-around shortcuts.

Numbering the Pages

Word numbers the pages in a document automatically, which is great, but if your document has a title page and table of contents and you want to start numbering pages on the fifth page, or if your document has more than one section, page numbers can turn into a sticky business.

The first thing to ask yourself is whether you've included headers or footers in your document. If you have, go to "Putting Headers and Footers on Pages," later in this part. It explains how to put page numbers in a header or footer.

Meantime, use the Insert⇨Page Numbers command to put plain old page numbers on the pages of a document:

1. Choose Insert⇨Page Numbers to open the Page Numbers dialog box.

Where the page number goes

2. In the Position and Alignment boxes, choose where you want the page number to appear. The lovely Preview box on the right shows where your page number will go.

3. Click to remove the check mark from the Show Number on First Page box if you're working on a letter or other document that usually doesn't have a number on page 1.

4. Click OK.

If you want to get fancy, I should warn you that it's easier to do that in headers and footers than it is in the Page Numbers dialog box. Follow the first three steps in the preceding list and click the Format button. Then, in the Page Number Format dialog box, choose an option:

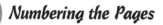
✦ **Number Format:** Choose a new way to number the pages if you want to. (Notice the *i, ii, iii* choice. That's how the start of books, this one included, is numbered.)

✦ **Include Chapter Number:** Click this check box if you want to start numbering pages anew at the beginning of each chapter. Pages in Chapter 1, for example, are numbered 1-1, 1-2, etc., and pages in Chapter 2 are numbered 2-1, 2-2, etc.

✦ **Chapter Starts with Style:** If necessary, choose a heading style from the drop-down list to tell Word where new chapters begin. Chapter titles are usually tagged with the Heading 1 style, but if your chapters begin with another style, choose it from the list.

✦ **Use Separator:** From the list, tell Word how you want to separate the chapter number from the page number. Choose the hyphen (1-1), period (1.1), colon (1:1), or one of the dashes (1—1).

✦ **Page Numbering:** This is the one that matters if you've divided your document into sections. Either start numbering the pages anew and enter a new page number to start at (probably 1), or else number pages where the previous section left off.

Page Number Format	? X
Number format:	1, 2, 3, … ▼
☑ Include chapter number	
Chapter starts with style	Heading 1 ▼
Use separator:	- (hyphen) ▼
Examples: 1-1, 1-A	
Page numbering	
○ Continue from previous section	
◉ Start at:	1 ▲▼
OK	Cancel

When you're done, click OK twice to number the pages and get back to your document.

To get rid of the page numbers if you don't like them, follow these steps:

1. Either choose View➪Header and Footer or double-click the page number in Page Layout view.

2. Click the Switch Between Header and Footer button, if necessary, to get to the footer.

3. Select the page number by clicking on it, and then press Del.

Suppose you have a title page and a table of contents on the first five pages of your document and want to start numbering pages on page 5. To do that, you have to divide your document into two sections. *See* "Dividing a Document into Sections" in Part III.

Opening an Existing Document

To open a document you've already created and named:

 1. Choose File⇨Open, press Ctrl+O, or click the Open button.

2. Find the folder that holds the file you want to open. To find the folder, click the Up One Level button, if necessary, to climb up the hierarchy of folders on your computer system, or else double-click folders to slide down the hierarchy of folders.

3. When you get to the folder the file is in, click on the file to select it.

4. Either double-click on the file you selected or click the Open button.

Up One Level   Look in Favorites   Add to Favorites

```
Open                                                    ? X
Look in:  Desktop Pub Docs        [icons]
  A dog's life              Welcome to New Orleans      Open
  Candy Production table    We're going global          Cancel
  Due to the unforunate incident                       Advanced...
  Merge cell table
  Practice table
  Preschool drawing
  rights of humanity
  Shading_Fire Alarm
  Soccer Standings
  The hoi polloi have a real treat

Find files that match these criteria:
File name:  [            ]    Text or property:  [      ]    Find Now
Files of type: Word Documents  Last modified: any time       New Search
12 file(s) found.
```

 If you're opening a document you worked on recently, it might be on the File menu. Check it out. Open the File menu and see if the document you want to open is one of the four listed at the bottom of the menu. If it is, click its name or press its number (1 through 4).

 To make it easier to open them, you can create "shortcuts" to the files and folders you use most often. To do that, choose File⇨Open and, in the Open dialog box, locate the file or folder to which you want to create a shortcut. Then select the file or folder and click the Open dialog box's Add to Favorites button. From the drop-down menu that appears, choose either the file or folder you selected or its parent folder. Next time you want to get to the folder or file in the Open dialog box, click the Look in Favorites button. A shortcut icon that represents the file or folder appears. Double-click the shortcut icon to get to the folder or open the file immediately. (To remove a shortcut icon, right-click it and choose Delete. By doing so, you delete the shortcut, not the file or folder itself.)

Opening a New Document

There are three ways to create a brand-new document:

✦ Choose File⇨New

✦ Press Ctrl+N

 ✦ Click the New button

If you opt for File⇨New, you see a dialog box with tabs and icons for creating documents from templates. A template is a ready-made layout you can use for formatting a document. By choosing a template for creating the new document, you don't have to do the formatting yourself. However, if you do want to do the formatting, double-click the Blank Document icon or click OK to open a new document.

Putting Headers and Footers on Pages

A *header* is a little description that appears along the top of a page so that the reader knows what's what. Usually, headers include the page number and a title. A *footer* is the same thing as a header, except it appears along the bottom of the page, as befits its name.

To add a header or a footer, follow these steps:

1. Choose View⇨Header and Footer.

2. Type your header in the box, or if you want a footer, click the Switch between Header and Footer button and type your footer.

3. Click the Close button.

While you're typing away in the Header or Footer box, you can call on most of the commands on the Standard and Formatting toolbars. You can change the text's font and font size, click an alignment button, and paste text from the Clipboard.

You can also take advantage of these buttons on the Header and Footer toolbar (if the buttons are too cryptic for your taste, you should know that you can get these same commands by choosing Insert⇨AutoText⇨Header/Footer):

Button	What It Does
Insert AutoText ▾	Opens a drop-down menu with options for inserting information about the document, including when it was last saved and printed, and who created it.
[#]	Inserts the page number.
[#+]	Inserts the number of pages in the entire document. On the right side of the sample header shown in the previous illustration, I pressed this button after pressing the Insert Page Number button and typing the word *of* and a space so that readers know the length of the document as well as what page they are on.
[#]	Opens the Page Number Format dialog box so that you can choose a format for the page number in the header of footer. *See* "Numbering the Pages" earlier in this part to find out how this dialog box works.
[📅] [🕐]	These buttons insert the date the document is printed and the time it is printed in the header or footer.
[📖]	Opens the Layout tab of the Page Setup dialog box so that you can tell Word that you want a different header and footer on the first page of the document, or that you want different headers and footers on odd and even pages (you might do this if you're printing on both sides of the page).
[📄]	Shows the text on the page so that you can see what the header or footer looks like in relation to the text.

(continued)

Button	What It Does
	Tells Word that you don't want this header or footer to be the same as the header or footer in the previous section of the document. To change headers or footers, you must divide a document into sections (*see* "Dividing a Document into Sections" in Part III).
	Switches between the header and the footer.
	Shows the header or footer in the previous and next section of a document that has been divided into sections.

Removing headers and footers is as easy as falling off a turnip truck:

1. Click View➪Header and Footer or double-click the header or footer in Page Layout View.

2. Select the header or footer.

3. Press Del.

 To remove the header and footer from the first page of a document, choose File➪Page Setup (or click the Page Setup button on the Header and Footer toolbar). In the Page Setup dialog box, click the Layout tab, click the Different First Page check box, and click OK.

Renaming a Document

If the name you gave to a document suddenly seems inappropriate or downright meaningless, you can rename it. Here's how:

1. Choose File➪Open, press Ctrl+O, or click the Open button.

2. In the Open dialog box, find the folder that holds the file you want to rename. You likely have to click the Up One Level button or double-click folders to find it.

3. Right-click on the file and choose Rename from the shortcut menu.

4. The old name is highlighted. Enter a new name in its place.

5. Click anywhere in the dialog box except on the renamed file.

6. Click Cancel to close the Open dialog box.

Saving a Document for the First Time

After you open a new document and work on it, you need to save it. As part of saving a document for the first time, Word opens a dialog box and invites you to give the document a name. So the first time you save, you do two things at once — you save your work and name your document.

To save a document for the first time:

1. Choose File⇨Save, press Ctrl+S, or click the Save button.

Up One Level

Save As	? X

Save in: Birds of the World

~$issor-Tailed Flycather
African Lovebird
Blackburnian Warbler
Black-Capped Chickadee
Great Bird of Paradise
Lady Amherst Pheasant
Leadbeater
Leadbeater's Cockatoo

Painted Bunting
Ruby-Throated Hummingbird
Scissor-Tailed Flycather
White-Breasted Nuthatch

Save
Cancel
Options...
Save Version...

File name: Full-Throated Bungadee

Save as type: Word Document

2. Find and select the folder that you want to save the file in. To do that, you might have to click the Up One Level button or double-click folders until you arrive at the right folder.

3. Word 97 suggests a name in the File Name box (the name comes from the first few words in the document). If that name isn't suitable, enter another. Be sure to enter one you will remember later.

4. Click the Save button.

Document names can be 255 characters long and can include all characters and numbers except these: / ? : * " < > |. They can even include spaces.

Saving a Document under a New Name

If you want to make a second copy of a document, you can do so by saving the first copy under a new name. When you're done, you will have two copies of the same file. To save a document under a new name:

1. Choose File⇨Save As.

2. Find and select a folder to save the newly named document in.

3. Give the document a new name in the File Name text box.

4. If you're also changing the type of file this is, click the Save as Type drop-down menu and choose the file type.

5. Click the Save button.

Saving a Document You've Been Working On

It behooves you to save your documents from time to time as you work on them. (No, *behooves* is not computer jargon. The word just means that you should.) When you save a document, Word takes the work you've done since the last time you saved your document and stores the work safely on the hard disk.

You can save a document in three different ways:

✦ Click the Save button

✦ Choose File⇨Save

✦ Press Ctrl+S

Save early and often. Make it a habit to click the Save button whenever you leave your desk, take a phone call, or let the cat out. If you don't save your work and there is a power outage or somebody trips over the computer's power cord, you lose all the work you did since the last time you saved your document.

Selecting Text in Speedy Ways

To move text or copy it from one place to another, you have to select it first. You can also erase a great gob of text merely by selecting it and pressing the Del key. So it pays to know how to select text. Here are some shortcuts for doing it:

To Select This	Do This
A word	Double-click the word.
A line	Click in the left margin next to the line.
Some lines	Drag the mouse over the lines or drag the mouse down the left margin.
A paragraph	Double-click in the left margin next to the paragraph.
A mess of text	Click at the start of the text, hold down the Shift key, click at the end of the text, and let up on the Shift key.
A gob of text	Put the cursor where you want to start selecting, press F8 or double-click EXT (it stands for Extend) on the status bar, and press an arrow key, drag the mouse, or click at the end of the selection.
Yet more text	If you select text and realize you want to select yet more text, double-click EXT on the status bar and start dragging the mouse or pressing arrow keys.
A document	Hold down the Ctrl key and click in the left margin, or else triple-click in the left margin, or choose Edit➪Select All.

If you have a bunch of highlighted text on-screen and you want it to go away but it won't (because you pressed F8 or double-clicked EXT to select it), double-click EXT again.

 After you press F8 or double-click EXT, all the keyboard shortcuts for moving the cursor also work for selecting text. For example, press F8 and press Ctrl+Home to select everything from the cursor to the top of the document. Double-click EXT and press End to select to the end of the line.

Spacing Lines

To change the spacing between lines, select the lines whose spacing you want to change or simply put the cursor in a paragraph if you're changing the line spacing in a single paragraph. If you're just starting a document, you're ready to go.

Choose Format➪Paragraph and pick an option in the Line Spacing drop-down list:

+ **Single, 1.5 Lines, Double:** These three options are quite up front about what they do.

+ **At Least:** Choose this one if you want Word to adjust for tall symbols or other unusual text. Word adjusts the lines but make sure there is, at minimum, the number of points you enter in the At box.

✦ **Exactly:** Choose this one and enter a number in the A̲t box if you want a specific amount of space between lines.

✦ **Multiple:** Choose this one and put a number in the A̲t box to get triple-, quadruple-, quintuple-, or any other-spaced lines.

Watch this box!⌐

Paragraph ? ✕

I̲ndents and Spacing | Line and P̲age Breaks

Alignment: Left ▼   O̲utline level: Body text ▼

Indentation
L̲eft: 0"   S̲pecial: (none) ▼   B̲y:
R̲ight: 0"

Spacing
B̲efore: 0 pt   Li̲ne spacing: Single ▼   A̲t:
Aft̲er: 0 pt

Single
1.5 lines
Double
At least
Exactly
Multiple

Preview

Tabs...   OK   Cancel

You can get a sneak preview of what your lines look like by glancing at the Preview box. Click OK when you've made your choice.

To quickly single-space text, select it and press Ctrl+1. To quickly double-space text, select and press Ctrl+2.

You might notice the B̲efore and Aft̲er boxes in the Spacing area on the I̲ndents and Spacing tab of the Paragraph dialog box. Use these boxes if you want blank space to be inserted automatically between paragraphs. But I must warn you that, to Word's mind, a heading is also a paragraph, so if you put space between paragraphs, you may get strange blank spaces around your headings. And if you put space before *and* after paragraphs, you'll get twice the amount of space between paragraphs that you bargained for. The B̲efore and Aft̲er boxes are for use with styles, when a certain style of paragraph is always preceded by or followed by a specific amount of space.

Spell-Checking (And Grammar-Checking) a Document

As you must have noticed by now, red wiggly lines appear under words that are misspelled, and green wiggly lines appear under words and sentences that Word thinks are grammatically incorrect. Correct spelling and grammar errors by right-clicking them and choosing an option from the shortcut menu. If the red or green lines annoy you, choose Tools⇨Options, click the Spelling & Grammar tab, and click to remove the check marks from Check Spelling As You Type or Check Grammar as You Type.

That's the one-at-a-time method for correcting misspelled words and grammatical errors. You can also go the whole hog and spell- or grammar-check an entire document or text selection by starting in one of these ways:

✦ Choose Tools⇨Spelling and Grammar

✦ Press F7

✦ Click the Spelling and Grammar button

You see the Spelling and Grammar dialog box. Spelling errors appear in red type in this dialog box. Grammatical errors are colored green.

Spelling and Grammar: English (United States)	? X
Not in Dictionary:	
There once was a man from Calcutta Who spoke with a terrible stutta	Ignore / Ignore All / Add
Suggestions:	
suttee / stutter / statue / state / stout / statute	Change / Change All / AutoCorrect
☑ Check grammar Options... Undo	Cancel

Correcting misspellings

Here are your options for handling red spelling errors:

✦ **Not in Dictionary:** Shows the word, in context, that was spelled incorrectly. You can click the scroll arrows in this box to see preceding or following text.

✦ **Suggestions:** Provides a list of words to use in place of the misspelling. Click the word that you think should replace the one that has been misspelled in the document.

✦ **Ignore:** Ignores the misspelling, but stops on it again if it appears later in the document.

✦ **Ignore All:** Ignores the misspelling wherever it appears in the document. Not only that, it ignores it in all your other open documents.

✦ **Add:** Adds the word in the Not in Dictionary box to the words in the dictionary that Microsoft Word deems correct. Click this button the first time that the spell-checker stops on your last name. By clicking this button, you add your last name to the spelling dictionary.

✦ **Change:** Click this button to insert the word in the Suggestions box in your document in place of the misspelled word.

✦ **Delete:** The Delete button appears where the Change button is when the Spell-Checker finds two words in a row ("the the," for example). Click Delete to remove the second word.

✦ **Change All:** Changes not only this misspelling to the word in the Suggestions box, but all identical misspellings in the document.

✦ **AutoCorrect:** Adds the suggested spelling correction to the list of words that are corrected automatically as you type them (*see* "Correcting Typos on the Fly" in Part V).

✦ **Undo:** Goes back to the last misspelling you corrected and gives you a chance to repent and try again.

You can click outside the Spelling dialog box and fool around in your document, in which case the Ignore button changes names and becomes Resume. Click the Resume button to start the spell-check again.

Suppose you have a bunch of computer code or Esperanto that you would like the spell-checker to skip and not waste time on. To keep the spell-checker from working on text, select the text, choose Tools⇨Language⇨Set Language, choose (no proofing) at the top of the scroll box, and click OK.

You probably shouldn't trust your smell-checker, because it can't catch all misspelled words. If you mean to type **middle** but type **fiddle** instead, the spell-checker won't catch the error because fiddle is a legitimate word. The moral is: If you're working on an important document, proofread it carefully. Don't rely on the spell-checker to catch all your smelling errors.

Fixing grammar errors

Word's Grammar Checker is theoretically able to correct grammatical mistakes in a document. Personally, I think the thing is useless and don't recommend using it. And I'm not just saying that because I'm an editor and writer and I (supposedly) have mastered grammar. I just think that a machine can't tell what's good writing and what isn't. Period.

Anyhow, grammar errors appear in green in the top of the Spelling and Grammar dialog box, as shown in this figure.

Click the following buttons to fix errors with the robo-grammarian:

Spelling and Grammar: English (United States)	? X
Punctuation:	
"For breakfast", he said, "Give me ba-ba-ba-bread With ba-ba-ba-ba-ba-ba butta!!!"	Ignore / Ignore All / Next Sentence
Suggestions:	Change
✓ Check grammar Options... Undo	Close

+ **Suggestions**: Lists ways to correct the error. Click the correction you want to make.

+ **Ignore:** Lets the error stand in your document.

+ **Ignore All:** Ignores this and all other identical grammar errors in this document and all others that are open.

+ **Next Sentence:** Ignores the error and takes you to the next sentence in the text.

+ **Change:** Replaces the error with what is in the Suggestions box.

+ **Undo:** Reverses your most recent correction.

Symbols and Special Characters

You can decorate your documents with all kinds of symbols and special characters — a death's head, a smiley face, the Yen symbol. To insert a symbol, click where you want it to go and do the following:

1. Choose Insert➪Symbol. The Symbol dialog box opens.

2. Click in the Font drop-down list to choose a symbol set.

3. When you choose some fonts, a Subset drop-down menu appears. Choose a subset name from the list to help locate the symbol you are looking for.

4. Click a symbol. When you do so, you see a bigger picture of it on-screen.

5. Click Insert.

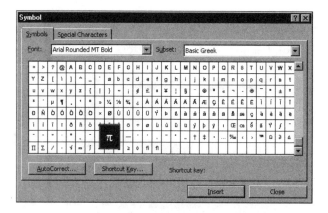

The symbol you choose is placed in your document, but the Symbol dialog box stays open so that you can select another symbol. Select another one, or click Close or press Esc when you are done.

You can also choose special characters and unusual punctuation from the Special Characters tab of the Symbol dialog box.

Also in the Insert dialog box is the AutoCorrect button, which you can click to open the AutoCorrect dialog box and add the symbol you clicked on to the list of symbols that Word inserts automatically (*see* "Correcting Typos on the Fly" in Part V for the details). You can also click the Shortcut Key button to assign a keyboard shortcut to the symbol you clicked on (*see* "Customizing Word 97," also in Part V).

Undoing a Mistake

Fortunately for you, all is not lost if you make a big blunder in Word 97, because Word 97 has a thing called the Undo command.

This command "remembers" your last 99 editorial changes and puts them on the Undo drop-down menu. As long as you catch your error before you do five or six new things, you can "undo" your mistake. There are two ways to undo:

✦ Choose Edit⇨Undo. This command changes names, depending on what you did last. Usually, it says Undo Typing, but if you move text, for example, it says Undo Move. Anyhow, select this command to undo your most recent action.

✦ Click the Undo button to undo your most recent change. If you made your error and went on to do something else before you caught it, click the down arrow next to the Undo button. You'll see a menu of your last six actions. Click the one you want to undo or, if it isn't on the list, click the down-arrow on the scroll bar until you find the error, and then click on it. However, if you do this, you also undo all the actions on the Undo menu that are above the one you're undoing. For example, if you undo the 98th action on the list, you also undo the 97 before it.

What if you commit a monstrous error but can't correct it with the Undo command? You can try closing your document without saving the changes you made to it. As long as you didn't save your document after you made the error, the error won't be in your document when you open it again — but neither will the changes you want to keep.

Viewing Documents in Different Ways

In word processing, you want to focus sometimes on the writing, sometimes on the layout, and sometimes on the organization of your work. To help you stay in focus, Word offers different ways of viewing a document:

✦ **Normal view:** Choose View⇨Normal or click the Normal View button (in the lower-left corner of the screen) when you want to focus on the words. Normal view is best for writing first drafts and proofreading.

✦ **Online Layout view:** Choose View⇨Online Layout or click the Online Layout View button to make looking at the document on-screen easier.

✦ **Page Layout view:** Choose View⇨Page Layout or click the Page Layout View button to see the big picture. You can see graphics, headers, and footers, and even page borders in Page Layout view. Rulers appear on the window so that you can pinpoint where everything is.

✦ **Outline view:** Choose <u>V</u>iew⇨<u>O</u>utline or click the Outline View button to see how your work is organized. In Outline view, you see only the headings and the first lines of paragraphs. To see a document in Outline view, you must have assigned heading styles to headings in the document. *See* "Outlines for Seeing the Big Picture" in Part V.

TIP To keep text from straying off the right side of the screen in Normal view, you can tell Word to "wrap it" so that you see all the text, no matter how long the lines in the document are. To wrap text, choose <u>T</u>ools⇨<u>O</u>ptions, click the View tab, and click the <u>W</u>rap to Window check box in the Window part of the tab. If you choose this option, just remember that the document on-screen is not the same as the one you print, because lines break in different places on-screen than they do on paper.

Working on Many Documents at Once

In Word, you can work on more than one document at the same time. You can even work in two different places in the same document (the next entry in this book tells how). All this magic is accomplished through the <u>W</u>indow menu.

To see how the <u>W</u>indow menu commands work, suppose for a moment that you're working on four poems — "Love," "Despair," "Hope," and "How I Yearn." It's the twilight hour and you're ready to compose, but you can't decide which poem to work on, so you open all four documents and wait for inspiration to strike.

When it does strike, you select the <u>W</u>indow menu and, depending on your mood, you choose one of the four documents listed at the bottom of the menu. Alternatively, you can put all four documents on-screen at once by choosing <u>W</u>indow⇨<u>A</u>rrange All. To go from one poem to the next, either click in a new window pane or press Ctrl+F6.

Love

When my lips for tender kisses long

Despair

Barren is the earth on which we toil!

Hope

I went awalking in the green, green woods

How I Yearn

How I yearn for the green days when my youth

Suppose you're feeling sentimental and want to close the "Hope," "Despair," and "How I Yearn" windows to concentrate on "Love." To do that, click the Minimize button of the window panes you don't want to see anymore. By doing so, you remove the other documents from the screen. Click the Restore button (the one in the middle with a square on it) to enlarge the window you want to work on to full-screen size.

To see a window you have minimized, open the Window menu again and choose it from the menu. When you minimize a window pane, you don't close the document. It's still there in case you need it.

Working in Two Places in the Same Document

You can open a window on two different places at once in a document. Here's one reason you might do this: You are writing a long report and want the introduction to support the conclusion, and you also want the conclusion to fulfill all promises made by the introduction. That's difficult to do sometimes, but you can make it easier by opening the document to both places and writing the conclusion and introduction at the same time.

There are two ways to open the same document to two different places: by opening a second window on the document or by splitting the screen.

Opening a second window

To open a second window on a document, choose Window⇨New Window. Immediately, a second window opens up and you see the start of your document.

✦ If you select the Window menu, you'll see that it now lists two versions of your document, number 1 and number 2 (the numbers appear after the filename). Choose number 1 to go back to where you were before.

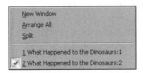

✦ You can move around in either window as you please. When you make changes in either window, you make them to the same document. Choose the File⇨Save command in either window and you save all the changes you made in both windows. The important thing to remember here is that you are working on a single document, not two.

✦ When you want to close either window, just click its Close button (be sure to choose the document's Close button, not Word 97's). You go back to the other window, and only one version of your document appears on the <u>W</u>indow menu.

Splitting the screen

Splitting a window means to divide it into north and south halves. To do that, choose <u>W</u>indow⇨<u>S</u>plit. A gray line appears on-screen. Roll the mouse down until the gray line is where you want the split to be, and click. You'll get two screens split down the middle:

What Happened to the Dinosaurs?

Science offers many reasons for the decline of the dinosaur. This paper will prove beyond the shadow of a doubt that the huge beasts were not done in by climactic changes, as present theory holds. On the contrary, the dinosaur evolved into those creatures who sing every morning in the trees outside our windows. They evolved into birds.

In Conclusion...

In conclusion, we can see that the dinosaurs were not done in by climatic changes, as present theory holds. Oh no. Oh no indeed. They evolved into those marvelous egg-laying creatures who sing in the morning. They became our feathered friends the birds.

Now you have two windows and two sets of scroll bars along the right side of the screen.

✦ Use the scroll bars to move up or down on either side of the split, or press PgUp or PgDn, or press arrow keys. Click the other side if you want to move the cursor there.

✦ When you tire of this schizophrenic arrangement, choose <u>W</u>indow⇨Remove S<u>p</u>lit or drag the gray line to the top or bottom of the screen.

 You can also split a screen by moving the mouse cursor to the top of the scroll bar on the right. Move it just above the arrow. When it turns into a funny shape, something like a German cross, click and drag the gray line down the screen. When you release the mouse button, you have a split screen.

Zooming In, Zooming Out

Eyes were not meant to stare at computer screens all day, which makes the Zoom command all the more valuable. Use this command freely and often to enlarge or shrink the text on your screen and preserve your eyes for important things, like gazing at the horizon.

There are two ways to give this command:

✦ Click the down arrow in the Zoom Control box on the Standard toolbar (the box on the right side that shows a number followed by a percent sign) and choose a magnification percentage from the drop-down list.

✦ Click inside the Zoom Control box, type a percentage of your own, and press Enter.

Enter or choose a zoom percentage here.⌐

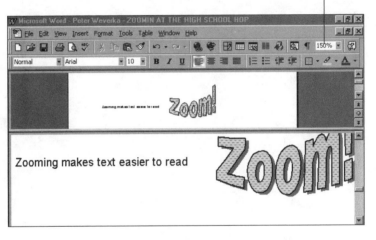

Zooming makes text easier to read

Sometimes it pays to shrink the text way down to see how pages are laid out. For instance, after you lay out a table, shrink it way down to see how it looks from a bird's-eye view.

Formatting Documents and Text

Half the work in word processing is getting the text to look good on the page. "Appearances are everything," Oscar Wilde remarked. The appearance of your documents should make as good an impression as their words, and that is what Part III is all about.

In this part . . .

✔ Changing the look of text

✔ Using the Style Painter, applying styles, and using other techniques to format text quickly

✔ Putting newspaper-style columns in documents

✔ Changing page margins, indentations, and tab settings

✔ Numbering lines and headings

Adding Bold, Italic, Underline, and Other Effects

It's easy to embellish text with **boldface,** *italics,* <u>underlines,</u> and other font styles and text effects. You can do it with the Formatting toolbar or by way of the Format⇨Font command. First the Formatting toolbar:

✦ **Boldface:** Click the Bold button (or press Ctrl+B) and start typing. If you've already entered the text, select the text first and then click Bold or press Ctrl+B. Bold text is often used in headings.

✦ **Italics:** Click the Italic button (or press Ctrl+I). Select the text first if you've already entered it. Italics are used to show emphasis and also for foreign words such as *voilà, gung hay fat choy,* and *Que magnifico!*

✦ **Underline:** Click the Underline button (or press Ctrl+U). Select the text first and then click the button if you've already typed the text. You can also get double underlines with the Format⇨Font command.

The second way to get boldfaced, italicized, and underlined text is to choose Format⇨Font. When the Font dialog box appears, choose options from the Font style scroll list.

┌Looky here to see the results. ┌Choose font styles.

┌Choose underline options. │Choose text effects.┐

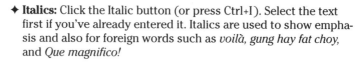

The Font dialog box offers many other options for embellishing text. They are shown in the following illustration. By choosing combinations of font styles and text effects, you can create interesting but sometimes unreadable letters and words.

Underline: Word 97 offers many ways to underline words and letters.

Strikethrough: I'm told that lawyers use the strikethrough style to show where text has been struck from legal contracts.

Double strikethrough: For all I know, egotistical lawyers, if there are any, use the double strikethrough style.

Superscript: Used to mark footnotes in text, in math and scientific formulas ($E = MC^2$), and in ordinal numbers (1st, 2nd, 3rd).

Subscript: Used in chemistry equations (H_2O).

Shadow: Makes the letters appear to cast a shadow.

Outline: Makes the letters appear in outline form.

Emboss: Makes the letters appear to stand up from the paper.

Engrave: Makes the letters look as though they were carved in stone.

Small caps: Used for time designations ("Columbus arrived in America on October 9 in AD 1492 at 11:30 A.M."). Not all fonts can produce small capital letters.

All caps: YOU KNOW WHAT THIS DOES, I TRUST.

Hidden: Keeps text from being printed or displayed (*see* "Hidden Text and Secret Messages" in Part VII).

It's easy to overdo it with text effects. Use them sparingly. When it comes to text effects, a little goes a long way.

Centering, Justifying, and Aligning Text

All you have to do to align text in a new way is select the text and either click an Alignment button on the Formatting toolbar or press a keyboard shortcut:

Button	Button Name	Keyboard Shortcut	What It Does
	Align Left	Ctrl+L	Lines up text along the left margin.
	Center	Ctrl+E	Centers text, leaving space on both sides.
	Align Right	Ctrl+R	Lines up text along the right margin.
	Justify	Ctrl+J	Lines up text on both the left and right margins.

Text is aligned with respect to the left and right *margins,* not the left and right sides of the page. This illustration may give you a clearer idea of the alignment options:

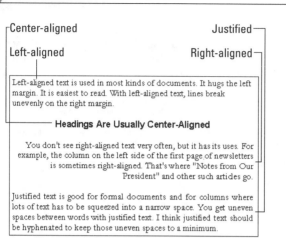

Changing the Font of Text

Font is the catchall name for type style and type size. When you change fonts, you choose another style of type or change the size of the letters. Word 97 offers a whole bunch of different fonts. You can see their names by clicking the down arrow next to the Font menu and scrolling down the list. Fonts with *TT* beside their names are *TrueType* fonts. These fonts look the same on-screen as they do when printed on paper.

To change the font:

1. Select the text or place the cursor where you want the font to change.

2. Click the down arrow on the Font menu.

3. Scroll down the list of fonts, if necessary.

4. Click a font name.

Word 97 puts all the fonts you've used so far in the document at the top of the Font menu to make it easier for you to find the fonts you use most often.

To change the size of letters:

1. Select the letters or place the cursor where you want the larger or smaller letters to start appearing.

2. Click the down arrow on the Font Size menu.

3. Scroll down the list if you want a large font.

4. Click a point size — 8, 12, 36, 48, and so on.

You can also change font sizes quickly by selecting the text and pressing Ctrl+Shift+< or Ctrl+Shift+>, or by clicking in the Font Size menu, entering a point size yourself, and pressing Enter.

Type is measured in *points*. A point is ¹/₇₂ of an inch. The larger the point size, the larger the letters. Business and love letters usually use 10- or 12-point type. For headings, choose a larger point size. In this book, first-level main headings are 18-points high and are set in the Cascade Script font. The text you are reading is Cheltenham 9-point font.

When you open a brand-new document and start typing, does the text appear in your favorite font? If it doesn't, you can make the font you use most often the default font:

1. Choose Format⇨Font.

2. Choose the font in the dialog box.

3. Click the Default button.

4. Click Yes when Word 97 asks you if this font really should be the default font.

Creating Numbered and Bulleted Lists

Numbered lists are invaluable in manuals and books like this one that present a lot of step-by-step procedures. Use bulleted lists when you want to present alternatives to the reader. A *bullet* is a black filled-in circle or other character.

Simple numbered and bulleted lists

The fastest, cleanest, and most honest way to create a numbered or bulleted list is to enter the text without any concern for numbers or bullets. Just press Enter at the end of each step or bulleted entry. When you're done, select the list and click either the Numbering or Bullets button on the Formatting toolbar.

Another way to create a numbered list is to type the number 1, press the spacebar, add a period, type the first entry in the list, and press Enter to get to the next line and type the second entry. As soon as you press Enter, Word inserts the number 2 and formats the list for you. Keep typing list entries and Word keeps right on numbering and formatting the list.

Ending and continuing lists

To end a numbered or bulleted list and tell Word that you want to go back to writing normal paragraphs, get to the Bullets and Numbering dialog box either by choosing Format⇨Bullets and Numbering or by right-clicking and choosing Bullets and Numbering from the shortcut menu. In the dialog box, click the Numbered or Bulleted tab, if necessary, select None, and then click OK.

Suppose you want a numbered list to pick up where a list you entered earlier ended. In other words, suppose you ended a four-step list a couple of paragraphs back and now you want the list to resume at step 5. In that case, open the Bullets and Numbering dialog box and click the Continue Previous List option button. The list will pick up where the previous numbered list in the document left off.

Also in the Bullets and Numbering dialog box is an option for starting a list anew. Choose Restart Numbering when Word insists on starting a list with a number other than 1 or when you want to break off one list and start another.

Constructing lists of your own

If you are an individualist and you want numbered and bulleted lists to work your way, start from the Bullets and Numbering dialog box (choose Format⇨Bullets and Numbering to get there). On the Bulleted and Numbered tabs, you can choose among different kinds of bullets and different numbering schemes.

If those choices aren't good enough for you, click the Customize button to open the Customize Numbered Lists or Customize Bulleted Lists dialog box. These dialog boxes offer opportunities for indenting numbers or bullets and the text that follows them in new ways. You can also choose fonts for the numbers and symbols for the bullets. Be sure to watch the Preview area of these dialog boxes. They show exactly what you are doing to your bulleted or numbered lists.

Watch this box! ─┐

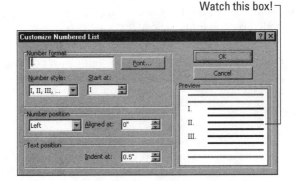

Dividing a Document into Sections

Every document has at least one *section*. That's why "Sec 1" appears on the left side of the status bar at the bottom of the screen. When you want to change page numbering schemes, headers and footers, margin sizes, and page layouts, you have to create a section break to start a new section. Word 97 creates one for you when you create columns or a table of contents.

To create a new section:

1. Click where you want to insert a section break.

2. Choose Insert⇨Break.

3. Tell Word 97 how to break the document. All four Section breaks options create a new section, but they do so in different ways:

- **Next Page:** Inserts a page break as well as a section break so that the new section can start at the top of a new page (the next one). Select this option to start a new chapter, for example.

[Break dialog box showing:]
Break
Insert
○ Page break   ○ Column break
Section breaks
● Next page   ○ Even page
○ Continuous   ○ Odd page
OK   Cancel

- **Continuous:** Inserts a section break in the middle of a page. Select this option, for example, if you want to change a header but don't want to insert a page break to do it.

- **Even Page:** Starts the new section on the next even page. This option is good for two-sided documents where the headers on the left- and right-hand pages are different.

- **Odd Page:** Starts the new section on the next odd page. You might choose this option if you have a book in which chapters start on odd pages (by convention, that's where they start).

4. Click OK.

In Normal View, you can tell where a section ends because `Section Break` and a double dotted line appear on-screen. The only way to tell in Page Layout View is to glance at the "Sec" listing on the status bar. To delete a section break, make sure you are in Normal View, click the dotted line, and press the Delete key.

Dropping In a Drop Cap

A *drop cap* is a large capital letter that "drops" into the text. Drop caps appear at the start of chapters in antiquated books, but you can find other uses for them. Here, a drop cap marks the A side of a list of songs on a homemade reggae tape.

> Bob Marley & the Wailers–Lively Up Yourself (1970)
> ❀Toots & the Maytals–Koo Koo (1968) ❀Gregory Issacs–
> Slavemaster (1971) ❀Junior Mervin–Police and Thieves
> (1973) ❀Lynton Kwesi Johnson–England Is a Bitch
> (1978)❀Lee Perry & the Upsetters–Stop the War in Babylon
> (1969)❀Militant Dread–Children of the Most High (1974) ❀
> Charlie Goetchius Dread–Them Na Downpress We Union (1982)

To create a drop cap:

1. Click anywhere in the paragraph whose first letter you want to "drop."

2. Choose Format⇨Drop Cap.

3. In the Drop Cap dialog box, choose which kind of drop cap you want by clicking a box. The <u>N</u>one setting is for removing a drop cap.

Drop Cap

Position

None   Dropped   In <u>M</u>argin

Options

<u>F</u>ont:
Desdemona

<u>L</u>ines to drop: 3

Distance from te<u>x</u>t: 0"

OK   Cancel

4. Choose a font from the <u>F</u>ont drop-down list. You should choose one that's different from the text in the paragraph. You can come back to this dialog box and get a different font later, if you wish.

5. In the <u>L</u>ines to Drop scroll box, choose how many text lines the letter should "drop on."

6. Keep the 0 setting in the Distance from Te<u>x</u>t box unless you're dropping an *I, 1,* or other skinny letter or number.

7. Click OK.

If you're not in Page Layout View, a dialog box asks whether you want to go there. Click Yes. You see your drop cap in all its glory.

The drop cap appears in a text frame. To change the size of the drop cap, you can tug and pull at the sides of the box (by dragging the handles with the mouse). However, you're better off choosing Format⇨<u>D</u>rop Cap again and playing with the settings in the Drop Cap dialog box.

Formatting a Document

A well-formatted document says a lot to the reader about how much thought and care was put into the work. If you're involved in any endeavor in which appearances count, it serves you well to go to the extra effort of making your documents look good. Word 97 offers a bunch of tools for formatting documents, some of them very complex. This section describes them.

You should double-check the words before you start formatting a document. It's easier to find mistakes and correct errors in raw text than it is to find and correct them in text that has been gussied up with different fonts and point sizes.

Fast formatting with the Format Painter

The fastest way to format a document is with the Format Painter. You can use this tool to make sure that the headings, lists, text paragraphs, and whatnot in your document are consistent with one another.

To use the Format Painter, follow these steps:

1. Click on the text whose formats you want to apply throughout your document. For example, if your document is a report with first-, second-, and third-level heads, format a first-level head so that it looks just right and click on it.

2. Double-click the Format Painter button. The mouse pointer changes into a paintbrush icon.

3. Find the text you want to copy the format to, click the mouse button, and roll the mouse pointer over it as though you were selecting it. When you're done, the text takes on the new formats.

4. Keep going. Find every place in your document that you can copy this format to and baste it with the Format Painter. You can click the scroll bar and use keyboard commands to move through your document.

5. Click the Format Painter button when you're done.

Using styles for consistent formatting

If you have a little more time on your hands, and if you really want the characters, headings, paragraphs, lists, and whatnot in your document to be consistent, use Word 97's style feature. The really neat thing about styles is that if you decide that a given style doesn't look right after you format a document, you can change it and have Word 97 instantly modify all paragraphs in your document to which you've assigned the given style.

To start with, every document has five default styles — one character style and four paragraph styles. You can see the default styles by pulling down the Style menu on the Formatting toolbar. *Paragraph styles,* which are marked by the paragraph symbol on the Style menu, determine the formatting of entire paragraphs. Create and use *character styles* as a means of changing fonts and type sizes quickly in Word. Character styles are marked with an underlined *a.* As you can see, Word gives a glimpse of what each style looks like on the Style menu.

Heading 1

Heading 2

Heading 3

Normal

Default Paragraph Font

Heading 1 style

Heading 2 style

Heading 3 style
Normal style
Default paragraph style

Creating a new style

You can create new styles and add them to the Style menu in two ways: with the Format⇨Style command and directly from the screen. First, the directly-from-the-screen method, which you can use to create paragraph styles:

1. Click on a paragraph whose formatting you would like to turn into a style and apply to other paragraphs in your document. Remember, a heading is also a paragraph as far as Word 97 is concerned, so if you're creating a style for a heading, click on the heading.

2. Click in the Style menu box and type a name for the style. Choose a meaningful name that you will remember.

3. Press Enter.

When you create a new style from scratch with the Format⇨Style command, it takes a bit longer, but you can be very precise about the style and its formatting.

1. Choose Format⇨Style.

2. Click the New button.

3. Fill in the New Style dialog box. As you do so, keep your eyes on the Preview box. It shows you what your new style will look like in a document.

- **Name:** Enter a name for the style. The name you enter will appear on the Style menu.

- **Style Type:** Click the down arrow and choose Character if you're creating a style for characters rather than paragraphs. If you often use an exotic font, you can create a style for it and simply click the style name on the Style menu instead of going to the trouble of formatting the characters in the document.

- **Based On:** If your new style is similar to one that is already on the menu, click here and choose the style to get a head start on creating the new one.

- **Style for Following Paragraph:** Choose a style from the drop-down list if the style you're creating is always followed by an existing style. For example, a new style called "Chapter Title" might always be followed by a style called "Chapter Intro Paragraph." If that were the case, you would choose "Chapter Intro Paragraph" from this drop-down list.

- **Add to Template:** Adds the style to the document's template so that other documents based on the template you are using can also make use of the new style.

- **Automatically Update:** Normally when you make a formatting change to a paragraph, the style assigned to the paragraph does not change at all, but the style does change if you check this box. By checking this box, you tell Word to alter the style itself each time you alter a paragraph to which you've assigned the style. With this box checked, all paragraphs in the document that were assigned the style are altered each time you change a single paragraph that was assigned the style.

- **Format:** This is the important one. Click the button and make a formatting choice. Word 97 takes you to dialog boxes so that you can create the style.

- **Shortcut Key:** Opens a dialog box so that you can apply the new style simply by pressing a shortcut key combination.

4. Click OK to close the New Style dialog box.

5. Click Apply to format the paragraph.

Applying a style to text and paragraphs

After you create a style and add it to the Style menu, applying it is as easy as pie:

1. Click on the paragraph you want to apply the style to. If you're applying a character style, select the letters whose formatting you want to change.

2. Click the down arrow on the Style menu to see the list of styles. Besides names, look at the icons, fonts, and alignment symbols to make sure you are choosing the right style.

3. Click on a style name.

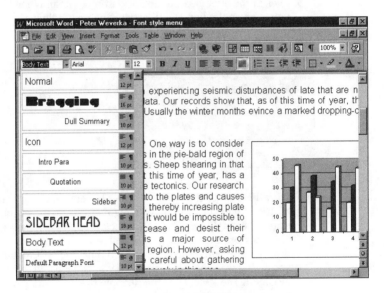

You can also take the long way around by choosing Format⇨Style, choosing a style from the Styles list in the Style dialog box, and clicking Apply.

In a document to which a lot of styles have been applied, it is sometimes hard to tell which style is which. To make that easier, choose Tools⇨Options, click the View tab in the Options dialog box, click the up arrow in the Style area width box a few times, and click OK. Back in your document, you see the names of the styles you applied on the left side of your screen.

Modifying a style

What if you decide at the end of an 80-page document that all 35 introductory paragraphs to which you've assigned the "Intro Para" style look funny? You can change them instantaneously. You can reformat the paragraph so that it looks right and have Word 97 also change the other paragraphs in the document to which you have assigned the same style. Here's how:

1. Click on any paragraph or group of characters to which you've assigned the style you want to change.

2. Reformat the paragraph or characters.

3. Click in the Style box on the Formatting toolbar. When you do so, you click on the name of the style you are modifying.

4. Press Enter. The Modify Style dialog box appears:

> **Modify Style**　　　　　　　　　　**? ✕**
>
> Style:　**Intro Para**
>
> Do you want to:
> ⦿ Update the style to reflect recent changes?
> ○ Reapply the formatting of the style to the selection?
>
> ☐ Automatically update the style from now on
>
> 　　　　　　　　　[OK]　[Cancel]

5. Click the Update the Style to Reflect Recent Changes? radio button. While you're here, you might also click the Automatically Update the Style from Now On check box. By clicking this box, you tell Word to alter the style itself — and all the paragraphs that were assigned the style — each time you reformat a paragraph that was given this style. (If you change your mind about modifying the style, click the Reapply the Formatting of the Style to the Selection? radio button.)

6. Click OK.

If you've devised a tortuously complicated style and want to change it, use the Modify Style dialog box. Choose Format⇨Style and click the Modify button in the Style dialog box. If the Modify Style dialog box looks familiar, that's because it is identical to the New Style dialog box you used to create the style in the first place. Change the settings, click OK, and click Apply to apply the new style throughout your document.

Using styles from the Style Gallery

The rogues' gallery of product designers who work at Microsoft knew that you would need a lot of different styles to do your work, so they invented the Style Gallery, a collection of templates that you can use to format documents.

The templates in the Style Gallery are the same ones you see when you choose File⇨New to open a new document.

A *template* is an assortment of different styles. New documents have the Normal template, the one that offers only five styles — Default Paragraph, Heading 1, Heading 2, and so on. Templates in the Style Gallery offer far more styles than that. And these styles were invented by pros, so they look good for the most part.

To add styles from a template in the Style Gallery to the styles you're already using in your document:

1. Choose Format⇨Style Gallery.

2. From the Template list, choose a template that most nearly describes what your document is and see what happens to your document in the wide-screen Preview Of box.

3. Click the Example check box to get a better look at what the template you chose has to offer.

4. Click the Style Samples check box. The Preview Of box shows the names of the styles in the template and how the styles are formatted.

5. After you play around with Style Gallery for a while and find a template that suits you, click OK.

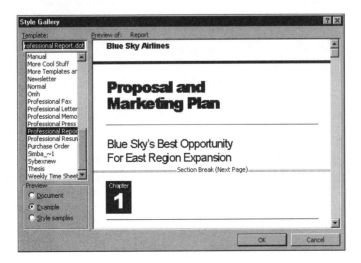

Indenting Paragraphs and First Lines

An *indent* is the distance between a margin and the text. Word 97 offers a handful of different ways to change the indentation of paragraphs.

The fastest way is to use the Increase Indent and Decrease Indent buttons on the Formatting toolbar to move the paragraph away from or toward the left margin:

1. Click in the paragraph whose indentation you want to change. If you want to change more than one paragraph, select them.

2. Click one of the buttons:

- **Increase Indent:** Indents the paragraph from the left margin by one tab stop (you can also press Ctrl+M).

- **Decrease Indent:** Moves the paragraph back toward the left margin by one tab stop (you can also press Ctrl+Shift+M).

You can also change indentations by using the ruler to "eyeball it." This technique requires some dexterity with the mouse, but it allows you to see precisely where paragraphs and the first lines of paragraphs are indented.

1. Choose View⇨Ruler, if necessary, to put the ruler on-screen.

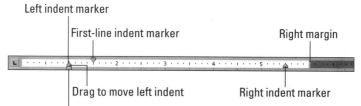

Left indent marker

First-line indent marker

Right margin

Drag to move left indent

Right indent marker

Drag to move paragraph and first line

2. Select the paragraph or paragraphs whose indentation you want to change.

3. Slide the indent markers with the mouse:

- **First-line indent marker:** Drag the down-pointing arrow on the ruler to indent the first line of the paragraph only.

- **Left indent marker:** This one, on the bottom-left side of the ruler, comes in two parts. Drag the arrow that points up, but not the box underneath it, to move the left margin independently of the first-line indentation. To move the left indentation *and* the first-line indentation relative to the left margin, slide the box. Doing so moves everything on the left side of the ruler.

- **Right indent marker:** Drag this one to move the right side of the paragraph away from the right margin.

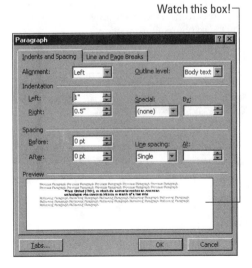

You can create neat effects by dragging the first-line indent marker toward the left margin to create *hanging indents.* In fact, Word 97 creates hanging indents automatically for bulleted and numbered lists. Notice where the first-line indent marker is on the ruler in the following illustration.

Highlights of Rosenda Monteros's marvelous film career include these credits:
- ♦ *White Orchid* (1954), in which the actress bewitches an American archeologist who comes to Mexico in search of a lost tribe.
- ♦ *The Magnificent Seven* (1961), in which the actress steals the heart of a gringo gunman come to save her village from marauders.

If you're not one for "eyeballing it," use the Format⇨Paragraph command to indent paragraphs:

1. Choose Format⇨Paragraph or double-click the Left or Right indent marker on the ruler.

2. Choose options in the Indentation area.

3. Click OK.

Watch this box!⌐

The Indentation options are self-explanatory. As you experiment, watch the Preview box — it shows exactly what your choices will do to the paragraph. In the Special drop-down list, you can choose Hanging to create a hanging indent or First Line to indent the first line from the left margin. Enter a measurement in the By box to say how far you want these indents to travel. Did you notice that Alignment drop-down list in the upper-left corner? You can even align paragraphs from this dialog box.

Numbering the Headings in a Document

In scholarly papers and formal documents, the headings are sometimes numbered so that cross-references and commentary can refer to them by number as well as by name. The Format⇨Bullets and Numbering command makes numbering the headings in a document very easy. The beauty of this command is that Word renumbers the headings automatically if you remove a heading or add a new one.

To use the Format⇨Bullets and Numbering command, you must have assigned heading styles to your document. First-level heads are given top billing in the numbering scheme. Subheadings get lower billing.

To number the headings in a document:

1. Switch to Outline view by clicking the Outline View button in the lower-left corner of the screen.

2. Click a Show Heading button (1 through 8) so you can see only the headings in Outline view. ("Outlines for Organizing Your Work" in Part V explains Outline view.)

3. Select the headings you want to number.

4. Choose Format⇨Bullets and Numbering.

5. Click the Outline Numbered tab in the Bullets and Numbering dialog box.

6. Click a numbering scheme in the Outline Numbered tab. Notice that some choices place words as well as numbers or letters before headings.

7. Click the Customize button if you want to devise your own numbering scheme or put a word before all headings. You can even choose new fonts for headings. If you experiment, be sure to watch the Preview box to see what kind of damage you're doing. Click OK when you're done experimenting.

8. Click OK to close the Bullets and Numbering dialog box.

If you regret having numbered the headings in your document, either choose Edit➪Undo Bullets and Numbering (or press Ctrl+Z), or go back to the Outline Numbered tab and choose None.

Numbering the Lines in a Document

As every legal secretary and lawyer knows, the lines in a legal contract have to be numbered. You can number lines very easily with Word 97. The numbers appear in the margin.

1. If you want to number the lines in one section only, place the cursor in that section. To number lines starting at one place, put the cursor where you want to start numbering. To number all the lines in the document, it doesn't matter where you place the cursor.

2. Choose File➪Page Setup.

3. In the Page Setup dialog box, click the Layout tab.

4. Click the Line Numbers button.

5. In the Line Numbers dialog box, click the Add Line Numbering check box.

6. Choose options from the Line Numbers dialog box:

- **Start At:** Enter the number to begin counting with if you want to begin with a number other than 1.

- **From Text:** Determines how far the numbers are from the text. The larger the number you enter, the closer the numbers appear to the left side of the page.

- **Count By:** All lines are numbered, but by choosing a number here you can make numbers appear at intervals. For example, entering **5** makes intervals of five (5, 10, 15, and so on) appear in the margin.

- **Numbering:** In legal contracts, the numbers begin anew on each page, but you can start numbering at each section or number all lines in the document consecutively.

7. Click OK.

8. Back on the Layout tab of the Page Setup dialog box, choose an Apply To option from the drop-down list. If you're numbering only a section, choose This Section. Otherwise, choose Whole Document to number all the lines or This Point Forward to number lines starting at the cursor.

9. Click OK.

To remove line numbers, follow steps 1 through 5 of the preceding set of instructions, but this time remove the check mark from the Add Line Numbering check box. Then click OK and click OK again in the Page Setup dialog box.

You can see line numbers only in Page Layout View. Even at that, you may have to scroll to the left with the scroll bar along the bottom of the screen to see them.

Putting Newspaper-Style Columns in a Document

Columns look great in newsletters and similar documents. And you can pack a lot of words in columns. With columns, you can present more than one document on a single page so that readers have a choice of what they read.

Before you put text in newspaper-style columns, write it. Take care of the spelling, grammar, and everything else, because it is hard to make text changes to words after they've been arranged in columns.

Sometimes it is easier to create columns by creating a table or by using tabs instead, especially when the columns refer to one another. In a two-column résumé, for example, the left-hand column often lists job titles ("Facsimile Engineer") whose descriptions are found directly across the page in the right-hand column ("I photocopied stuff all day long"). Creating a two-column résumé with Word's Format⇨Columns command would be futile because it is impossible to make the columns line up. Each time you add something to the left-hand column, everything "snakes" — it gets bumped down in the left-hand column and the right-hand column as well.

There are two ways to create columns: with the Columns button on the toolbar and with the Format⇨Columns command. Format⇨ Columns gives you considerably more leeway because the Columns button only lets you create columns of equal width. To use the Columns button:

1. Either select the text to be put in columns or simply place the cursor in the document to "columnize" all the text.

2. Switch to Page Layout view by clicking the Page Layout View button or choosing View⇨Page Layout. You can see columns only in Page Layout view.

3. Click the Columns button on the toolbar. A menu drops down so that you can choose how many columns you want.

4. Click one, two, three, or four columns.

Very likely, your columns don't look so good. It's hard to get it right the first time. You can drag the column border bars on the ruler to widen or narrow the columns:

Drag to change column width.

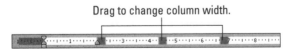

However, it's much easier to choose Format⇨Columns and play with options in the Columns dialog box. If you want to start all over, or if you want to start from the beginning with the Columns dialog box, here's how:

1. Select the text to be put in columns, or put the cursor in the section to be put in columns, or place the cursor at a position in the document where columns are to start appearing.

2. Switch to Page Layout view if you're not already there.

3. Choose Format⤇Columns.

4. Choose options from the Columns dialog box. As you do so, keep your eye on the Preview box in the lower-right corner:

Watch this box!⌐

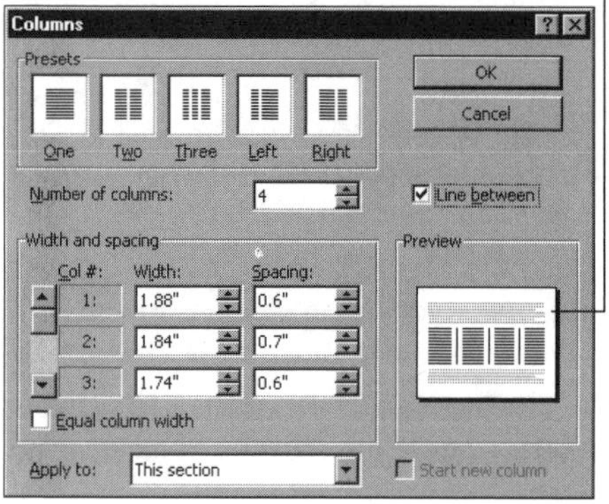

- **Presets:** Click a box to choose a preset number of columns. Notice that, in some of the boxes, the columns aren't of equal width. Choose <u>O</u>ne if you want to remove columns from a document.

- **Number of Columns:** If you want more than three columns, enter a number here.

- **Line <u>B</u>etween:** Click this box to put lines between columns.

- <u>C</u>ol #: If your document has more than three columns, a scroll bar appears to the left of the <u>C</u>ol # boxes. Scroll to the column you want to work with.

- **W<u>i</u>dth:** Change the width of each column by using the W<u>i</u>dth boxes.

- **<u>S</u>pacing:** Determines how much blank space appears to the right of the column.

- **Equal Column Width:** Click this box to remove the check mark if you want columns of various widths.

- **<u>A</u>pply To:** Choose which part of the document you want to "columnize" — selected text, the section the cursor is in, this point forward in your document, or the whole document.

- **Start New Column:** This box is for putting empty space in a column, perhaps to insert a text box or picture. Place the cursor where you want the empty space to begin, open the Columns dialog box, click this check box, and choose This Point Forward from the Apply to drop-down menu. Text below the cursor moves to the next column.

5. Click OK.

TIP Faster ways to "break" a column in the middle and move text to the next column are to press Ctrl+Shift+Enter or choose Insert⇨Break and click the Column Break button.

As you format your multicolumn newsletter or incendiary pamphlet, click the Print Preview button early and often. The best way to see what a multicolumn document really looks like is to see it on the Print Preview screen.

See also Part VI for information about including pictures and text boxes in columns.

Setting Up and Changing the Margins

Margins are the empty space between the text and the left, right, top, and bottom edges of a page. Headers and footers are printed in the top and bottom margins, respectively.

Don't confuse margins with indents. Text is indented from the margin, not from the edge of the page. If you want to change how far a paragraph is indented, use the ruler or the Format⇨Paragraph command and change its indentation.

To change the margin settings:

1. Place the cursor where you want to change margins, if you are changing margins, in the middle of a document. Otherwise, to change the margins in the entire document, it doesn't matter where you place the cursor.

2. Choose File⇨Page Setup.

3. Choose the settings on the Margins tab, and watch the Preview box to see what your choices do:

   • **Top, Bottom, Left, Right, Inside, Outside:** Set the top, bottom, left and right, or inside and outside, margins. (You see the Inside and Outside settings if you click the Mirror Margins check box.)

   • **Gutter:** Allows extra space on the inside margin for documents that will be bound. Click the up arrow to see what binding looks like as it eats into the left side of the page and alters the left margin.

   • **Header:** Makes the top margin lower so that you can fit two or three lines in headers.

   • **Footer:** Makes the bottom margin higher for footers.

   • **Apply To:** Choose Whole Document to apply your settings to the entire document, This Section to apply them to a section, or This Point Forward to change margins for the rest of a document. When you choose This Point Forward, Word 97 creates a new section.

   • **Mirror Margins:** Makes room for the binding on pages that will be bound and on which text will be printed on both sides.

4. Click OK.

You can change the top and bottom margins with the horizontal ruler in Page Layout view. Simply drag the margin bar up or down.

 If you don't care for the Word 97 default margin settings, make your own in the Page Setup dialog box and click the Default button. Henceforth, new documents that you open will have *your* margin settings.

Working with the Ruler

The ruler along the top of the screen is there to help you change and identify margins, tab settings, and indents, as well as place graphics and text boxes. (If you don't see it, choose View⮕Ruler.)

In Page Layout view, there is a similar ruler along the left side of the screen.

 You can change the unit of measurement that is shown on the rulers. Choose Tools⮕Options, click the General tab, and choose Inches, Centimeters, Points, or Picas from the Measurement Units drop-down list. Here is what the horizontal ruler looks like with point measurements:

| ⌐ ⋯ ·36· ⋯ ·72· ⋯ 108 ⋯ 144 ⋯ 180 ⋯ 216 ⋯ 252 ⋯ 288 ⋯ 324 ⋯ 360 ⋯ 396 ⋯ |

See also "Indenting Paragraphs and First Lines," "Setting Up and Changing the Margins," and "Working with Tabs" in this part to learn how to do those things with the rulers.

Working with Tabs

A *tab stop* is a point on the ruler around which or against which text is formatted. When you press the Tab key, you advance the text cursor by one tab stop. Tab stops are set at half-inch intervals on the ruler, but you can change that if you want to.

You can also change the type of tab. By default, tabs are left-aligned, which means that when you enter letters after you press the Tab key, the letters move toward the right in the same way that they move toward the right when text is left-aligned. However, Word 97 also offers right, center, and decimal tabs. The following illustration shows the differences between the tab settings. Notice the symbols on the ruler — they tell you what type of tab you are dealing with.

Left	Center	Right	Decimal
January	January	January	January
Oct.	Oct.	Oct.	Oct.
1234	1234	1234	1234
$45.95	$45.95	$45.95	$45.95
13,579.32	13,579.32	13,579.32	13,579.32

Tabs are a throwback to the days of the typewriter, when it was necessary to make tab stops in order to align text. Except for making leaders, everything you can do with tabs can also be done by creating a table — and it can be done far faster. All you have to do is align the text inside the table and then remove the table borders. See "Constructing the Perfect Table" in Part VI.

To change tabs or change where tabs appear on the ruler:

1. Click in the box on the left side of the ruler to get different tab settings. As you click, the symbols change, as shown:

Symbol	Tab Type
L	Left-aligned tab
⊥	Center-aligned tab
⌐	Right-aligned tab
⊥.	Decimal tab

2. When you come to the symbol that represents the type of tab you want, click on the ruler where you want to put a tab stop. You can click as many times as you want and enter more than one kind of tab.

Here is a ruler with all four kinds of tabs on it:

You can move a tab on the ruler simply by dragging it to a new location. Text that has been aligned with the tab moves as well, if you select it first. To remove a tab, drag it off the ruler. When you remove a tab, the text to which it was aligned is aligned to the next tab stop on the ruler.

You can also make tab settings with the Tabs dialog box:

1. Place the cursor where you want your new tab settings to take effect. Or else select the text to which you want to apply your new tabs.

2. Choose Format⇨Tabs. You see the Tabs dialog box.

3. Enter a position for the first new tab in the Tab Stop Position box.

4. Choose an Alignment option. The Bar option places a vertical bar, or straight line, at the tab stop position. You can place numbers inside these bars, for example, to help line them up.

Tabs

Tab stop position: Default tab stops: 0.5"
5"

0.5"
2"
3.5"
5"

Alignment
- ○ Left   ● Decimal
- ○ Center   ○ Bar
- ○ Right

Leader
- ● 1 None   ○ 3 ------
- ○ 2 ....   ○ 4 ___

Tab stops to be cleared: 6", 7.56"

Set   Clear   Clear All

OK   Cancel

5. Choose a leader, if you want one. For example, if you choose 2, Word 97 places periods in the document whenever you press Tab at this setting. A *leader* is a series of identical characters. Leaders are often found in tables of contents — they are the periods between the table of contents entry and the page number it refers to.

6. Click the Set button.

7. Repeat steps 3 through 6 for the next tab setting and all other tab settings. If you change your mind about a setting, select it in the Tab Stop Position scroll box and click Clear. Click Clear All if you change your mind in a big way and want to start all over.

8. Click OK.

Sometimes it is hard to tell where tabs were put in the text. To find out, click the Show/Hide ¶ button to see the formatting characters, including the arrows that show where the Tab key was pressed.

Leaders are very elegant. For this illustration, I used left-aligned tab stops for the characters' names and right-aligned tab stops for the players' names. I included leaders so you can tell precisely who played whom.

| | 1 | | 2 | | 3 | | 4 | |

The Players

Romeo.................................McGeorge Wright
Juliet.................................Gabriela Hernandez
Mercutio...Chris Suzuki
Lady Capulet...........................Mimi Hornstein

Printing Your Documents

What is a document until you print it? Not much. It's like an idea that hasn't been written down or communicated to anyone yet. A document isn't worth much until you run it through the printer and put it on paper so that other people can read it.

Part IV explains how to print documents in Word 97. It describes how to print labels and addresses on envelopes, print on sheets of paper other than the standard $8^1/_2$ x 11, and set up the pages for printing. This part also tells you what to do if you just can't get your documents to print.

In this part . . .

✔ Seeing what you print before you print it

✔ Printing envelopes and address labels

✔ Printing on legal-size and odd-shaped paper

✔ Telling Word 97 how to print a document

✔ Solving problems with the printer

Previewing What You Print

Before you print a document, do yourself a big favor by *previewing* it. That way, you can catch errors before you send them through the printer and waste 1, 2, 5, or 20 sheets of paper.

To preview a document:

1. Put the document you're about to print on-screen.

2. Choose File⇨Print Preview or click the Print Preview button on the toolbar. A panoramic picture of your document appears on the Preview screen:

3. Use the buttons on the Preview screen to get a better look at your document:

- Click the Magnifier button to zoom in on a part of a page. When you click this button, a magnifying glass cursor appears. Click on the part of the document you want to examine. When you're done, click again to get back to the Preview screen.

- Click the One Page or Multiple Pages button to view one or several pages at once.

- Click the Zoom Control menu and either enter a percentage and press Enter or choose a different percentage from the menu to see more of a page. You can also click the Page Width setting to make the page wider on the Preview screen.

- Click the Shrink to Fit button, and Word 97 shrinks your document a bit. Choose this option if the last page only has a few lines of text and you want to save a piece of paper.

- The Full Screen button removes the menu bars and ruler so that you can really get the "big picture" of a page.

Prints the document   Shrinks document

Changes size on-screen | Enlarges Preview screen

Closes Preview screen

Shows | Displays
one page | rulers   Gets Help

| Microsoft Word - Peter Weverka - rights of humanity2 [Copy] |
| File Edit View Insert Format Tools Table Window Help |

DECLARATION
OF THE RIGHTS
OF HUMANITY

Zooms in   └─Shows many pages

4. Click <u>C</u>lose if you need to go back to the document and make changes; otherwise, click the Print button.

Printing Addresses on Envelopes

You don't have to address envelopes by hand, although it's often easier to do it that way. Here's how to print addresses and return addresses on envelopes:

1. Open the document that holds the letter you want to send and select the name and address of the person you want to send the letter to.

2. Choose <u>T</u>ools⇨<u>E</u>nvelopes and Labels. The Envelopes and Labels dialog box appears with the address you selected in the <u>D</u>elivery Address box. Your address should appear in the <u>R</u>eturn Address box (if it isn't there, see the Tip at the end of this entry to find out how to put it there).

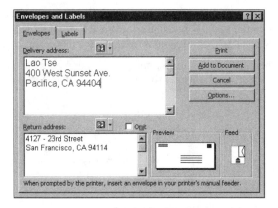

3. Change the Delivery Address or Return address, if necessary. Users of Outlook, people who have a personal address book, and subscribers to the Microsoft Network can click the Address Book button to get addresses.

4. Click the Omit check box if you don't want your return address to appear on the envelope.

 5. Click the Print button.

Two commands on the Envelopes tab tell Word 97 how your printer handles envelopes and what size your envelopes are.

Click the envelope in the Feed area to choose the right technique for feeding envelopes to your printer. Click one of the Feed Method boxes, click the Face Up or Face Down option button, and pull down the Feed From menu to tell Word 97 which printer tray the envelope is in or how you intend to stick the envelope in your printer. Click OK when you're done.

After you've fed the envelope to your printer, click in the Preview box on the Envelopes tab to tell Word 97 what size your envelopes are and choose other settings:

✦ **Envelope Size:** Pull down the menu and select the right size.

✦ **Delivery Point Bar Code:** Click here to put bar codes on the envelope and help the post office deliver the letter faster.

✦ **FIM-A Courtesy Reply Mail:** Click here to put Facing Identification Marks on the envelope. These marks, which tell letter-processing machines at the post office whether the envelope is face up, also help with the speedy delivery of mail.

✦ **Delivery Address:** Change the font of the delivery address and the address's position.

✦ **Return Address:** Ditto for the return address.

FIM marks ─┐   Bar codes ─┐

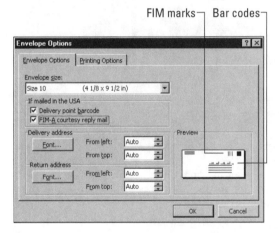

That Add to Document button on the Envelopes tab of the Envelopes and Labels dialog box creates a new section at the top of the document with the return and delivery address in it. In the new section, both addresses are formatted and made ready to go straight to the printer. Not everyone can take advantage of this feature. Click the Add to Document button only if you have a printer that can accept envelopes as easily as it can accept sheets of paper (I want one for my birthday).

To make your return address appear automatically in the Return Address box, choose Tools⇨Options, click the User Information tab, and enter your name and address in the Mailing Address box.

Printing on Different-Sized Paper

You don't have to print exclusively on standard 8½-x-11-inch paper; you can print on legal-size paper and other sizes of paper as well. A 'zine or newsletter with an unusual shape really stands out in a crowd and gets people's attention.

To change the size of the paper on which you intend to print a document:

1. Choose File⇨Page Setup.

2. Click the Paper Size tab.

```
┌─────────────────────────────────────────────────────────┐
│ Page Setup                                      [?][X]    │
│ ┌─────┬───────────┬─────────────┬────────┐               │
│ │Margins│ Paper Size │ Paper Source │ Layout │            │
│                                                           │
│  Paper size:                   ┌─Preview──────────┐       │
│  ┌──────────────────────┐▼     │                  │       │
│  │ Custom size          │      │                  │       │
│  Width:    ┌─────┐▲              │                  │      │
│            │5.6" │▼              │                  │      │
│  Height:   ┌─────┐▲              │                  │      │
│            │14.1"│▼              │                  │      │
│  ┌─Orientation─────────┐        │                  │      │
│  │ ┌──┐ ⊙ Portrait     │        │                  │      │
│  │ │ A│ ○ Landscape     │       └──────────────────┘      │
│  │ └──┘                │                                   │
│                    Apply to: ┌─────────────────┐▼         │
│                              │ Whole document  │          │
│                                                           │
│  ┌──────────┐            ┌──────┐  ┌────────┐             │
│  │ Default... │            │  OK  │  │ Cancel │           │
│  └──────────┘            └──────┘  └────────┘             │
└─────────────────────────────────────────────────────────┘
```

3. Choose a setting from the Paper Size drop-down list. If none of the settings suits you, enter your own settings in the Width and Height text boxes.

4. Choose an Apply To option:

- **Whole Document** for the entire document.

- **This Section** if your document has more than one section.

- **This Point Forward** to create a new section and change the paper size for the rest of the document.

5. Click OK.

If you keep legal-size paper in one tray of your printer and standard-size paper in another, for example, click the Paper Source tab in the Page Setup dialog box and change settings there. *See also* "'Land-scape' Document" in Part VI to learn how to print landscape, not portrait, documents.

Click the Default button in the Paper Size tab of the Page Setup dialog box if you want your choice of paper size to be the default — the choice that is made whenever you open a new document.

Printing a Document

The fastest way to print a document is to click the Print button on the Standard toolbar. Go this route if you want to print the entire thing from start to finish. (Before you print a document, however, you ought to "preview" it by pressing the Print Preview button or choosing File⇨Print Preview.)

To print part of a document, selected text in a document, the entire thing, or even unusual things like comments and summary text, follow these steps:

1. Choose File⇨Print (or press Ctrl+P) to open the Print dialog box.

Print	? X
Printer	
Name:	HP LaserJet IIIP ▼ Properties
Status:	Idle
Type:	HP LaserJet IIIP
Where:	LPT1: ☐ Print to file
Comment:	

Page range
○ All
○ Current page ○ Selection
◉ Pages: 1-12, 14-16, 20, 24
Enter page numbers and/or page ranges separated by commas. For example, 1,3,5–12

Copies
Number of copies: 1
☑ Collate

Print what: Document ▼ Print: All pages in range ▼
Options... OK Cancel

2. Enter the number of copies you want in the Number of Copies box.

3. Choose a Print Range option to tell Word 97 how much of the document to print:

- **All:** Prints the whole thing.

- **Current Page:** Prints the page where the cursor is.

- **Selection:** Prints the text that was selected.

- **Pages:** Prints certain pages only. Enter hyphens to designate the page range and commas, too, if you want to print more than one page range. For example, entering **1-4**, prints pages 1 through 4, but entering **1,4** prints those pages only.

4. Choose Print to Fi_l_e to copy the document to a print file. You might do this in order to take your document to a print shop and have it printed there. If you choose this option and click OK, the Print to File dialog box appears. Choose a name for the print file and click OK.

5. Click OK.

The Print dialog box also offers these options:

✦ **Colla_t_e:** If you're printing more than one copy of a document with many pages and you don't want the copies to be collated, click the Colla_t_e box to remove the check mark. If you were printing three three-page documents, for example, the pages would come out of the printer 111, 222, 333, instead of 123, 123, 123.

✦ **Print _W_hat:** Choose one of the admittedly strange options on the Print _W_hat drop-down menu to print the comments in your document, AutoText entries, examples of the styles you've used, key assignments you've used, or document property information.

✦ **P_r_int:** Choose Odd Pages or Even Pages from the P_r_int menu to print those pages only. This is the option to choose if you want to print on both sides of the paper. Print the odd pages, turn the pages over and feed them to your printer, and then print the even pages.

Printing sections in a document can be very problematic, especially if the pages in each section are numbered differently. To print an entire section, enter an **s** and then the section number in the Print dialog box's Pages box. For example, to print Section 6, enter **s6**. To print pages within a section, enter a **p** and then the page number. For example, to print page 4 through 10 in Section 6, enter **p4s6-p10s6**.

Printing Labels

You can print pages of labels in Word 97, and single labels, too. Needless to say, printing labels makes mass mailing and bulk mailing much easier. If you have Avery brand or MACO standard labels, you've got it made because Word 97 is all set up to work those labels. This section explains how to print single labels and print labels for mass mailings.

As much as it pains me to write this, you should probably get a box of Avery or MACO standard labels if you want to print labels with Word 97 (although some label manufacturers give Avery equivalent numbers). You can tell Word 97 what your labels look like by fiddling with the settings, but one peek at the Preview box that you use to do so will probably discourage you from even thinking about it:

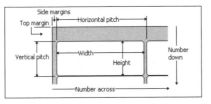

Printing labels one at a time

To print mailing labels, follow these steps:

1. Open the document that contains the address of the label you want to print and select the address.

2. Choose Tools⇨Envelopes and Labels.

3. Click the Labels tab. The address appears in the Address box. If the name or address is wrong, now's the time to fix it. If you're printing labels with your return address on them, click the Use Return Address box or enter your return address. You can also click the Address Book button and get addresses that way.

4. Either click the Options button or click the sample label in the Label box. The Label Options dialog box appears.

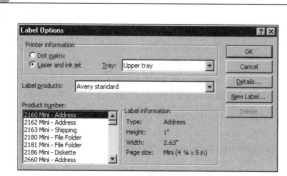

5. In the Printer Information area, click either Dot Matrix or Laser and Ink Jet to say which kind of printer you have. Then pull down the Tray menu and click the option that describes how you will feed the label to your printer.

6. Click the Label Products drop-down list and choose the brand or type of labels you have.

You may not have to choose Other if your labels don't fall into one of the dialog box's categories. You might be able to choose an Avery or MACO one similar to the labels you have (see step 7). If you do choose Other, click the Details button and use the Custom Information dialog box to explain, in 4,000 words or less, how your labels are laid out on the page.

7. In the Product Number box, click the Avery product you have. If you don't have Avery labels, click the various kinds of Avery labels and look in the Label Information box on the right to see if the Height, Width, and Page Sizes match those of the labels you have. If they do, you can choose an Avery label.

8. Click OK to go back to the Envelopes and Labels dialog box.

9. Choose a Print option:

- **Full Page of the Same Label:** Click this box if you want to print a pageful of the same label. Likely, you'd choose this option to print a pageful of your own return addresses. Click the New Document button after you make this choice. Word 97 creates a new document with a pageful of labels. Save and print this document.

- **Single Label:** Click this box to print one label. Then enter the row and column where the label is and click the Print button.

Printing labels for mass mailings

To print a mess of labels for mass or bulk mailings, Word 97 offers the Mail Merge Helper. To use this nifty tool, you can either enter the labels yourself one at a time or draw upon a mailing list that you or someone else already created. To draw upon a mailing list, however, the list must be in a table or a database format. *See* "Constructing the Perfect Table" in Part VI to learn how to turn a simple list into a table.

To use the Mail Merge Helper to create a file of address labels:

1. Open a new document and choose Tools⇨Mail Merge. The Mail Merge Helper opens.

2. Click the Create button and then click Mailing Labels in the drop-down list.

3. In the message box, click Active Window to add the labels to the new document you just opened.

4. Under step 2 in the Mail Merge Helper, click Get Data to see the menu of choices for getting the mailing label addresses:

- **Create Data Source:** Choose this option if you haven't yet entered the names and addresses for the labels. For the details of what to do after you choose this option, *see* "Churning Out Form Letters" in Part V.

- **Open Data Source:** Choose this option to get the names and addresses from a mailing list table that you or somebody else has already created. The instructions in the rest of this entry explain what to do if you make this choice.

- **Use Address Book:** Choose this option to get the names and addresses from the Personal Address Book, Outlook Address Book, or Schedule+ Address Book.

- **Header Options:** Choose this sophisticated option to get headers (data categories) from one file and the raw data from another. (To find out about this option, choose Help⇨Contents and Index, click the Index tab, and enter **header sources** in box 1.)

5. In the Open Data Source dialog box, find the document that holds the table with your addresses, click it, and click the Open button.

6. In the message box that appears, click the Set Up Main Document button.

7. Choose options in the Label Options dialog box. This is where you tell Word what size the labels are. If these options are new to you, consult steps 5 through 7 in the preceding section of this book, "Printing labels one at a time." Click OK when you're done. The Create Labels dialog box appears.

8. In this dialog box, you create the sample label that Word 97 will use as model for all the labels on the list. To do that, place the cursor in the Sample Label box where you want the addressee's name to go, click Insert Merge Field, and choose the name from the top of the drop-down list. It appears in the Sample Label box.

9. Press Enter to go to the next line in the Sample Label box, click Insert Merge Field again, and enter the next line in the address, probably the street number and name. Press Enter again. Keep doing this until you enter the entire address.

10. Fix all punctuation, remove empty spaces and enter blank ones where necessary, put a blank space before the zip code (to separate it from the two-letter state abbreviation), and do whatever else is necessary to clean up the address. In my case, Microsoft Weird 97 put mysterious *M*s in the list and I have to delete them.

Whatever you do, don't erase the angle brackets (<<>>) or press Enter inside them. The brackets are there to mark off the parts of the address.

11. You can enter a postal bar code with the Insert Postal Bar Code button and drop-down list.

12. Click OK.

13. Back in the Mail Merge Helper, click the Merge button. You see the Merge dialog box.

14. Make sure the Don't Print Blank Lines When Data Fields Are Empty box is checked. This prevents blank lines from appearing in your labels.

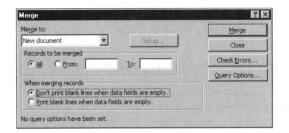

15. Click the <u>M</u>erge button. Word 97 generates the mailing labels in a file called Labels1, and you get something like this:

Ms. Gladys Yee 1293 Durham Lane Osterville, MA 02655	Ms. Esther Harmony 2601 Estner Rd. Osterville, MA 02655
Ms. Melinda Sings 2789 Estner Rd. Osterville, MA 02655	Mr. Rupert S. Stickenmud 119 Scutter Lane Osterville, MA 02655

 16. Choose <u>F</u>ile⇔<u>S</u>ave, press Ctrl+S, or click the Save button and save your label file under a new name in the Save As dialog box.

17. Now that your labels are on disk, put a blank sheet of labels in the printer and print your new labels.

Solving Problems with the Printer

Occasionally, you try to print a document and get this disconcerting message or one like it:

In David Letterman fashion, here is a top-ten list of things to do when you can't print a document or a document doesn't print correctly:

10. Is text running off the page? You may have attempted to print on paper that is the wrong size. Choose <u>F</u>ile⇔Page Set<u>u</u>p, click the Paper <u>S</u>ize tab, and change the Pape<u>r</u> Size options.

9. Are your graphics not printing? Choose Tools⇨Options, click the Print tab, and click the Draft Output check box to remove the check mark.

8. Do you keep getting the same printer error message? You may have selected the wrong printer. Choose File⇨Print and choose another printer from the Name drop-down list. If that doesn't work, try reinstalling your printer with the Add New Hardware application in the Windows 95 Control Panel.

7. Do the gridlines appear in tables? That's because you haven't given your table borders or you're printing on a dot-matrix printer, which doesn't print table lines very well.

6. Have you loaded envelopes in the printer, but Word 97 still doesn't budge? Probably you put the envelopes in the wrong tray. Choose Tools⇨Envelopes and Labels, click the Envelopes tab, click the envelope inside the Feed box, and choose the correct method of loading envelopes in your printer.

5. Do fonts look different on-screen than they do on paper? Your printer might not be able to handle certain fonts, in which case you have to find substitutes among the TrueType fonts you have. TrueType fonts look the same on-screen as they do when printed. You can tell a TrueType font on the Font menu because it has a *TT* next to its name.

4. Are lines breaking in strange places? Your margins may be too wide. Change the margin settings.

3. Do you keep seeing the `There is an error writing to your printer` message? You may have sent too many print jobs to the printer. Wait for your printer to digest what you've already sent it and try again.

2. Does Word 97 tell you `There was an error writing to` blah blah blah? You may be out of paper. Or maybe the printer cables aren't hooked up correctly.

1. Are you getting nothing but error messages? See if the printer is turned on. If it's not on, you can't print.

Telling Word 97 How to Print Documents

Before you can print a document, Word 97 has to know where the paper is and what kind of printer you're using. Windows 95 probably told its cousin Word 97 what kind of printer you have when you installed your printer, but it doesn't hurt to check. And if you keep different paper in different trays, you need to tell Word 97 where the right size paper is.

1. Choose File⇨Print or press Ctrl+P.

2. In the Print dialog box, click the down-arrow on the Name drop-down menu and choose a printer, if necessary.

3. Click the Properties button.

4. On the Paper tab, choose which size paper you're using or, if you're printing an envelope, which size envelope you intend to print on.

5. From the Paper Source drop-down list, choose the right tray, or choose a method of feeding envelopes to your printer if you're printing an envelope.

6. Click OK to get back to the Print dialog box and click OK again.

Making Your Work Go Faster

Computers are supposed to make your work easier and faster. And if you can cut through all the jargon and technobabble, they can really do that.

Part V explains shortcuts and commands that will help you become a speedy user of Word 97. Everything in this part of the book was put here so that you can get off work an hour earlier and take the slow, scenic route home.

In this part . . .

✓ Moving around quickly in long documents

✓ Creating form letters by merging letters with names and addresses in a database table

✓ Linking files

✓ Entering data quickly with forms

✓ Using master documents and outlines to organize your work

✓ Customizing Word 97 so that it works for you

Bookmarks for Hopping Around

Instead of pressing PgUp or PgDn or clicking the scroll bar to thrash around in a long document, you can use bookmarks. All you do is put a bookmark in an important spot in your document that you'll return to many times. When you want to return to that spot, choose Insert⇨Bookmark, double-click the bookmark in the Bookmark dialog box, and click Cancel.

This mystery writer, true to the craft, wrote the end of the story first and used bookmarks to jump back and forth between the beginning and end to make all the clues fit together:

To place a bookmark in a document:

1. Click where you want the bookmark to go.

2. Choose Insert⇨Bookmark (or press Ctrl+Shift+F5).

3. Type a descriptive name in the Bookmark Name box. You cannot include spaces in bookmark names.

4. Click the Add button.

To go to a bookmark:

1. Choose Insert⇨Bookmark (or press Ctrl+Shift+F5).

2. Double-click the bookmark or select it and click the Go To button.

3. Click Cancel or press Enter.

You can arrange bookmarks in the list in alphabetical order or by location in the document by choosing Name or Location at the bottom of the Bookmark dialog box. Click the Hidden bookmarks check box to see cross-references in the Bookmark Name box, although hidden bookmarks appear as code and don't tell you much about what they are or where they are in the document.

To delete a bookmark, select it in the Bookmark dialog box and click the Delete button.

Churning Out Form Letters

Thanks to the miracle of computing, you can churn out form letters in the privacy of your home or office, just like the big companies do. To create form letters, you complete three steps:

1. Create the *main document,* the document with the actual text of the letter.

2. Create the *source document,* the document with the names, addresses, and any other text that differs from letter to letter. You can use an address list that you have already created and saved as the source document. To use that list, however, it must be in a table or database format. *See* "Constructing the Perfect Table" in Part VI to learn how to turn a simple list into a table.

3. Merge the two documents to generate the form letters.

TIP

Before you generate the form letter, write a first draft. You need to know precisely where the information that varies from recipient to recipient — the names and addresses, for example — goes before you start generating the letter.

To generate form letters:

1. Open a new document by clicking the New button, pressing Ctrl+N, or choosing File➪New. With the File➪New command, you can choose one of the Word 97 letter templates for your form letter by choosing a template from the Letters & Faxes tab.

2. Choose Tools➪Mail Merge. The Mail Merge Helper dialog box appears.

3. Click the Create button and choose Form Letters from the drop-down list.

4. A message box asks if you want to create the form letters in the active document or in a new document. Click the Active Window button.

5. Under step 2 in the Mail Merge Helper, click Get Data to see the menu of choices for getting the mailing addresses for the letters:

- **Create Data Source:** Choose this option to enter the names and addresses now. The instructions in the rest of this entry explain what to do if you make this choice.

- **Open Data Source:** Choose this option to get the names and addresses for the form letters from a mailing list table that you or somebody else has already created. *See* "Printing Labels for Mass Mailings" in Part IV if you choose this option. The techniques for getting data from another source are the same whether you are creating labels or form letters.

- **Use Address Book:** Choose this option to get the names and addresses from the Personal Address Book, Outlook Address Book, or Schedule+ Address Book.

- **Header Options:** Choose this sophisticated option to get headers (data categories) from one file and the raw data from another. (To find out about this option, choose Help⇨Contents and Index, click the Index tab, and enter **header sources** in box 1.)

6. Choose Create Data Source. You see the Create Data Source dialog box. This is where you tell Word 97 which fields to include in the form letter. In computerese, a *field* is simply one piece of information. For example, your name and address include at least six fields: first name, last name, street number and name, city, state, and postal code.

7. In the Field Names in Header Row box, click on each field you *don't* need and then click the Remove Field Name button.

Carefully consider which fields your form letter requires, and look in the Field Names in Header Row box to see which fields you need. Likely, your form letter needs the FirstName, LastName, Address1, City, State, and PostalCode field.

8. To create a field of your own, type its name in the Field Name text box and click the Add Field Name button. If you were just creating an address list, you could get by with the fields I mentioned in step 7. However, your form letter likely needs other fields. For example, if you want to include a date — perhaps the recipient's birthday — you need to create a "birthday" field so that you can enter birthdays in your letter. Field names cannot have spaces in them.

9. Arrange the field names in the Field <u>N</u>ames in Header Row box in the order in which they will appear in your form letter. To do so, highlight a field and press one of the Move buttons to move the field to the right place.

10. Click OK to close the Create Data Source dialog box.

11. In the Save As dialog box, enter a name for the new document you are creating to save your form letters. If you have been following these steps to create labels, enter a name for the labels you are about to create. Then click <u>S</u>ave.

12. Word tells you that you need to add records to the data source document you just named. Click the Edit <u>D</u>ata Source button. The Data Form dialog box appears with the names of the fields you created in the Create Data Source dialog box.

13. Enter data in each field. If you need to leave a field blank, leave it blank — don't put any blank spaces in it.

14. Click the <u>A</u>dd New button to enter the next name and address. When you're done entering all of them, click OK.

Now you see the *main document* again. This is where you type the text of the form letter. If you followed my advice, you have a first draft to copy from. Now all you have to do is insert the fields in the correct places.

15. Start typing the letter. When you come to a place where you want to insert a field, click the Insert Merge Field button and choose the field from the list.

16. Keep typing and making field selections with the Insert Field Merge menu. Click the View Merged Data button from time to time to see how you are progressing. You can format the letter any way you wish. It will look something like this when you're done:

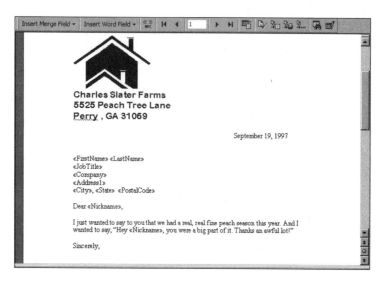

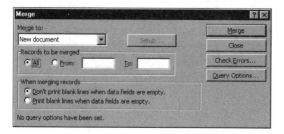

17. When you're done, click the Mail Merge Helper button.

18. In the now familiar Mail Merge Helper dialog box, click the Merge button. The Merge dialog box appears.

19. In the Merge dialog box, tell Word 97 how to merge the *data source* with the *main document:*

- **Merge To:** Choose New document to create a new file with all the form letters in it. If you're generating a lot of form letters, this file can get very large. Choose Printer to merge the names and addresses with the form letter as the form letters are printed. This choice requires less disk space. Choose Electronic mail if you are merging e-mail addresses with e-mail messages.

- **Records to Be Merged:** Click A̲ll, or else enter a record number in the F̲rom and T̲o boxes.

- **When Merging Records:** Make sure the D̲on't Print Blank Lines When Data Fields Are Empty check box is selected. That way, you keep blank lines from appearing in addresses.

- **Check E̲rrors:** Click this button and Word 97 reports errors as the files are merged. For example, it tells you when it can't find a match between the data source and a field in your form letter.

- **Query Options:** Opens a dialog box so that you can sort (rearrange) or filter (weed out) records. Click this option, for example, to merge the letters in a different order (perhaps in zip code order) or merge only addresses in a certain state or zip code.

20. Click M̲erge in the Merge dialog box.

21. If you chose to merge to the printer in step 19, the Print dialog box appears so that you can choose settings and print away. If you chose New document, Word 97 creates a new document with the name Form Letters1. Look over the form letters for mistakes and perhaps enter a few chummy, personal comments before you print the document.

22. Sign and mail the form letters. Use Elvis stamps if you can find them.

Correcting Typos on the Fly

Unless you or someone else has messed with the Word 97 Auto-Correct settings, the invisible hand of Word 97 corrects certain typos as you enter them. Try misspelling *weird* by typing *wierd* to see what I mean. Try entering two hyphens (- -) and you get an em dash (—). You can have Word 97 correct the typos you make often, and with a little cunning you can even use the AutoCorrect feature to enter long company names and hard-to-spell names on the fly.

To change the settings and make AutoCorrect work for you, choose T̲ools⇨AutoCorrect. The AutoCorrect dialog box appears.

✦ Remove the check marks from the AutoCorrect features you
don't want. For example, if you enter a lot of computer code in
your manuscripts, you don't necessarily want the first letter of
sentences to be capitalized automatically, so you should click the
Capitalize First Letter of Sentences check box to deselect it.

✦ If you want, remove the check mark from the Replace Text as You
Type box to keep Word's invisible hand from correcting capitalization and spelling idiosyncrasies as you enter them.

✦ Scroll through the list and take a look at the words that are
"autocorrected." If you don't want a word on the list to be
corrected, select it and click Delete.

✦ If a word that you misspell often isn't on the list, you can add it
to the list and have Word 97 correct it automatically. Enter the
misspelling in the Replace box, enter the right spelling in the
With box, and click the Add button.

✦ If you don't like one of the Word 97 replacement words, select the
word on the list, enter a new replacement word in the With box,
and click the Replace button.

Click OK when you're done.

The Spelling dialog box has an AutoCorrect button. Click it when
you're spell-checking a document to add the word you're correcting
to the list of words that are "autocorrected." The AutoCorrect
choice also appears on the shortcut menu when you right-click a
misspelled word.

If AutoCorrect frustrates you, you don't have to ditch it altogether. You can have Word make exceptions for the words, proper names, and abbreviations you use. For example, if you work for QUestData Corp., you can make Word allow that name to stand but still correct other instances when you type two capital letters at the start of a word. If you use a certain abbreviation often, you can add it to the list of abbreviations that Word 97 lets stand without starting the next word with a capital letter. Here's how:

1. Choose Tools⇨AutoCorrect.

2. Click the Exceptions button.

3. On the First Letter tab, enter abbreviations that you intend to use but that aren't on the list. Word capitalizes the first letter after a period, except in the cases of the abbreviations listed here.

4. On the INitial CAps tab, enter words or names with two capitals in a row that you want Word to let stand.

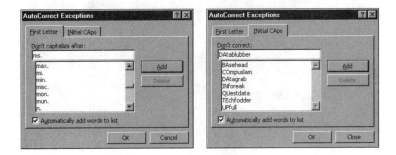

5. Click OK twice to get back to your document.

 With a little cunning, you can use AutoCorrect to enter long words, long e-mail addresses, and the like. Suppose you are writing the definitive work on Gaetano Donizetti, the Italian opera composer. To keep from having to type his long name over and over, choose Tools⇨AutoCorrect, enter **/gd** (or something similar) in the Replace box, enter the full name in the With box, and click Add. Now all you have to do is type **/gd** and a blank space, and AutoCorrect writes out the entire name. The catch is that you have to enter letters in the Replace box that you won't ever, ever, ever need to really use.

Customizing Word 97

You can make Word 97 work your way by fiddling with the commands in the Options dialog box. You can even put menu commands in different places and invent your own keyboard shortcuts for executing commands. *See also* "Rearranging the Toolbars," also in Part V, to learn how to make toolbars with your favorite command buttons on them.

 One glance at the ten tabs in the Options dialog box tells you that there is a lot to fiddle with. You can see this dialog box by choosing Tools⇨Options. If you decide to play around with these options, do so carefully because you might change a setting, forget where you changed it, and not be able to change it back again.

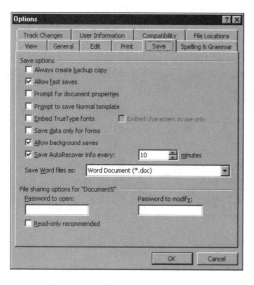

Changing the menu commands

You can decide for yourself which menu commands appear on which menus. You can also add macros, fonts, AutoText entries, and styles to menus. Doing so is easy, and if you make a mistake and want to go back to the original menus, that is easy, too.

 The quickest (but scariest) way to remove a command from a menu is to press Ctrl+Alt+hyphen. When the cursor changes into an ominous black bar, simply select the menu command you want to remove. Press Esc, by the way, if you decide after you press Ctrl+Alt+hyphen that you don't want to remove menu commands.

A more precise way to remove menu commands or alter the menus is use the Commands tab of the Customize dialog box:

1. Choose Tools⇨Customize.

2. Click the Commands tab.

3. If you want to make the menu changes to a template other than Normal.dot or the template you are working in, choose the template in the Save In drop-down list.

4. In the Categories list, select the menu you want to change. If you're adding a macro, font, AutoText entry, or style to a menu, scroll to the bottom of the Categories list and select it. The commands that are on the menu you chose appear in the Commands list on the right.

5. Choose the command you're changing in the Commands list.

6. What you do next depends on whether you want to remove the menu command, add it to a menu, or change its position on a menu. Changing menu commands requires moving the pointer out of the Customize dialog box and clicking on menus on the menu bar.

- **Removing:** To remove a menu command, move the pointer over the menu that holds the command you want to remove and click gently. That's right — click on the menu name as you normally would if you were pulling it down to choose one of its commands. When the menu appears, click the menu command you want to remove and drag it off the menu. You see a gray rectangle above the pointer and an *X* below it. Release the mouse button after you have dragged the menu command away from the menu.

- **Adding:** To add a menu command to a menu, drag it from the Commands list in the Customize dialog box and to the menu itself. As you do this, you see a gray rectangle above the pointer and a plus sign below it. Move the pointer over the menu to which you want to add the command. The menu appears. Gently drag the pointer down the menu to the spot where you want the command to be listed. A black line appears on the menu to show where your command will go. When the command is in the right spot, release the mouse button.

- **Changing position:** To change the position of a command on a menu, move the pointer out of the Customize dialog box and gently click on the menu whose command you want to move. Then drag the pointer up or down the list of commands. A black line shows where the command will move when you release the mouse button. When the black line is in the right spot, let go of the mouse button.

7. Click Close.

If you wish that you hadn't messed with the menus and want to repent, choose Tools➪Customize click the Commands tab, right-click on the name of the menu whose commands you fooled with, and choose Reset from the shortcut menu.

Changing the keyboard shortcuts

If you don't like Word 97 keyboard shortcuts, you can change them and invent keyboard shortcuts of your own. You can also assign keyboard shortcuts to symbols, macros, fonts, AutoText entries, and styles.

1. Choose Tools➪Customize.

2. Click the Keyboard button. You see the Customize Keyboard dialog box.

![Customize Keyboard dialog box]

Customize Keyboard

Categories:
File
Edit
View
Insert
Format
Tools
Table

Commands:
FileClose
FileCloseAll
FileCloseOrCloseAll
FileConfirmConversions
FileExit
FileFind
FileNew

Close
Assign
Remove
Reset All...

Press new shortcut key:
Ctrl+.

Currently assigned to:
[unassigned]

Current keys:

Description
Closes all of the windows of the active document

Save changes in:
Normal.dot

3. To make the changes to a template other than Normal.dot or the template you are working in, choose a template in the Sa<u>v</u>e Changes In drop-down list.

4. In the <u>C</u>ategories list, choose the menu in which you want to assign the keyboard shortcut. At the bottom of the list are the Macro, Font, AutoText, Style, and Common symbols categories.

5. Choose the command name, macro, font, AutoText entry, style, or symbol name in the C<u>o</u>mmands list.

6. Click in the Press <u>N</u>ew Shortcut Key box and type the keyboard shortcut. Press the actual keys. For example, if the shortcut is Ctrl+Z, press the Ctrl key and the Z key — don't type out **C-t-r-l-+-Z**.

If you try to assign one that is already assigned, the words `Currently assigned to` and a command name appear below the Press <u>N</u>ew Shortcut Key box. You can override the pre-assigned keyboard assignment by entering a keyboard assignment of your own.

7. Click the <u>A</u>ssign button.

8. When you're done, click the Close button.

9. Click Close in the Customize dialog box.

To delete a keyboard shortcut, display it in the C<u>u</u>rrent Keys box, click it to select it, and click the <u>R</u>emove button.

You can always get the old keyboard shortcuts back by choosing the Re<u>s</u>et All button in the Customize Keyboard dialog box. Click <u>Y</u>es when Word 97 asks whether you really want the old keyboard shortcuts back.

Entering Graphics and Text Quickly

Put the text and graphics you use often on the <u>I</u>nsert⇨AutoText list. That way, you can enter the text or graphics simply by clicking a few menu commands or by choosing names from a toolbar. Addresses and company logos are ideal candidates for the <u>I</u>nsert⇨AutoText list because they take so long to enter.

To see how AutoText works, choose <u>I</u>nsert⇨AutoText and slowly slide the cursor over the AutoText command categories. As you do so, you see lists of the generic words and phrases that the mighty Microsoft Corporation thinks you are likely to need. To enter one of these words or phrases in a document, all you have to do is click it.

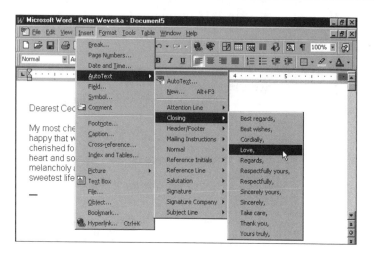

Creating your own AutoText entries

To create an AutoText entry:

1. Type the text or import the graphic.

2. Select the text or graphic.

3. Choose Insert⇨AutoText⇨New or press Alt+F3. The Create AutoText dialog box appears:

4. Type a name for the text or graphic in the text box and click OK.

You can also create a text entry by choosing Insert⇨AutoText⇨ AutoText. In the AutoCorrect dialog box, click the AutoText tab, and then type the word or phrase in the Enter AutoText Entries here box. Click OK when you're done.

Inserting an AutoText entry

The fastest way to insert an AutoText entry is to place the cursor where you want it to go and start typing the entry's name. Midway through, a yellow bubble appears with the entire entry. Press Enter at that point to insert the whole thing:

> All agree that the best circus in the world is the Fly [Flying Weverkas]

Another speedy way to insert AutoText entries is to type the entry's name and then press F3.

You can also enter text or a graphic from the Insert⇨AutoText list:

1. Place the cursor where you want the text or graphic to appear.

2. Choose Insert⇨AutoText⇨Normal. The Normal list is where the entries you made are shown.

3. In the Normal list, click the name of the AutoText entry that you want to insert.

Yet another way to insert an AutoText entry is to display the AutoText toolbar, click on the drop-down menu, and click on the entry.

To delete an AutoText entry, choose Insert⇨AutoText⇨AutoText, click the AutoText tab, click the entry you want to delete, and click the Delete button.

 Those yellow AutoText bubbles can be very annoying. They pop up in the oddest places. Try typing the name of a month, for example, to see what I mean. To keep the bubbles from appearing, choose Insert⇨AutoText⇨AutoText and click to remove the check mark from the Show AutoComplete Tips for AutoText and Dates check box.

Entering Information Quickly with Forms

A *form* is a means of soliciting and recording information. Besides creating paper forms, you can create computerized forms that make entering data easy. Designing computerized forms is a tricky business and is too complicated for this little book, but this entry will get you started.

Creating a paper form

To create paper forms, use commands on the Table menu. By shading cells, by merging cells, by drawing borders around different parts of the table, and by using different fonts, you can create a form like the one shown here. (*See* "Constructing the Perfect Table" in Part VI to learn how to work with tables.) In this illustration, the table is shown first with only the text and the gridlines. Borders and shading have been added to different parts of the final, completed table to make it look like a form.

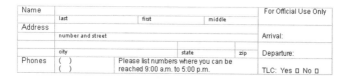

Creating a computerized form

A computerized form is an electronic version of a paper form. Computerized forms make entering data easier because the person who enters the data can only type in predefined areas — he or she can't erase the names of the fields where data is entered. If you were to turn the paper form in the previous illustration into a computerized form, you or someone else could then enter the data from the paper forms into a computer file very quickly and cleanly.

The first step to creating a computerized form is to design the form. Enter the names of the fields — the places where information goes — and leave empty spaces for the information itself. Instead of designing the computerized form from scratch, you can use a paper form you created with Microsoft Word.

After you have designed the form, you turn it into a template and tell Word 97 where the fields are. With that done, you choose File⇨New, choose the template you created for your new file, and open the file. Then you enter the raw data itself. You can only enter data in the predefined fields. When you are done, you have a file with all the data in it.

Here is how to create a computerized form:

1. Open a new document, or, if you have already designed a paper form, open the paper form. Label the fields appropriately and make sure there is enough room to enter the raw data you will enter later.

2. Choose File⇨Save As. You are going to save the document as a template.

3. Type a name for the template in the File Name box.

4. Click the Up One Level button until you get to the Templates folder.

5. Choose Document Template in the Save as Type drop-down list. The name of your template is given a *.dot* ending.

6. Click Save.

Now that the form is a template, you have to put input fields in it so that you can enter the raw data. A *field* is simply a piece of information. Input fields fall into three categories:

◆ **Text:** A text entry, such as a name, address, or telephone number

◆ **Check Box:** A "multiple choice," such as two or three check boxes, only one of which can be selected

◆ **Drop Down:** A drop-down menu of choices

To enter input field types, open the Forms toolbar. Do that by right-clicking on a toolbar and choosing Forms from the shortcut menu. To enter the input fields:

1. Go to the first place in the template where data is to be entered.

2. Click the Text Form Field, Check Box Form Field, or Drop-Down Form Field button on the Forms toolbar, depending on the type of field you need. When you do so, Word 97 puts shading on the form where the field is. (If you don't see the shading, click the Form Field Shading button on the Forms toolbar.)

3. Keep going down the template and entering form fields. In this form, I have entered 11 fields. The two in the lower-right corner are Check Box fields.

Name					For Official Use Only	
	last		first	middle		
Address					Arrival:	
	number and street					
	city		state	zip	Departure:	
Phones	( )	Please list numbers where you can be				
	( )	reached 9:00 a.m. to 5 p.m.			TLC: Yes ☐ No ☐	

Don't worry about the fields' length. Unless you click the Form Field Options button and change the settings, text of any length can be entered in input fields. However, you might change the length setting in a zip code field to keep anyone from inputting more than nine numbers, for example.

4. When you're done entering the input fields, click the Protect Form button. Now whoever enters the data on the form cannot disturb the field names. He or she can only type in the input fields.

5. Save the template and close it.

Now that you have the template, you can enter data cleanly in easy-to-read forms:

1. Choose File⇨New to open a new document to enter the data in.

2. Double-click the template you created.

3. Enter information in the input fields. Press the up or down arrow, or press Tab and Shift+Tab to move from field to field. You can also click on input fields to move the cursor there. Notice that you can't change the field labels.

4. When you're done, either print the document or save it.

Going Here, Going There in Documents

Word offers three very speedy techniques for jumping around in documents: the Select Browse Object button, the Edit⇨Go To command, and the document map.

"Browsing" around a document

A really fast way to move around quickly is to click the Select Browse Object button in the lower-right corner of the screen. When you click this button, Word presents ten "Browse by" icons:

Select the icon that represents the element you want to go to, and Word takes you there immediately. For example, click the Browse by Heading icon to get to the next heading in your document. After you have selected a "Browse by" icon, the navigator buttons — the double-arrows directly above and below the Select Browse Object button — turn blue. Click a blue navigator button to get to the next example or the previous example of the element you chose. For example, if you selected the Browse by Heading icon, all you have to do is click blue navigator buttons to get from heading to heading backwards or forwards in a document.

Going there fast

Another fast way to go from place to place in a document is to use the Edit⇨Go To command. Choose this command or press Ctrl+G to see the Go To tab of the Find and Replace dialog box:

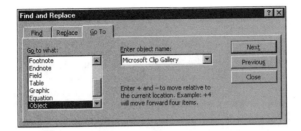

The Go to What menu in this dialog box lists everything that can conceivably be numbered in a Word 97 document, and other things, too. Everything you can get to with the Select Browse Object button, as well as lines, equations, and objects, can be reached by way of the Go To tab. Click a menu item and enter a number or choose an item from the drop-down list to go elsewhere.

Click the Previous button to go back to the footnote, endnote, comment, line, or whatever you just came from. You can press + or – and enter numbers to go backward or forward by one or several numbered items at once.

Hopping from place to place

Yet another way to hop from place to place is by turning on the document map. To do so, click the Document Map button or choose View➪Document Map. Everything in the document that hasn't been assigned the Normal style — headings, captions, and so on — appears along the left side of the screen. By placing the pointer on the text that doesn't fit on-screen, you can read it. Click the heading, captions, or whatever you want to go to, and Word 97 takes you there in the twinkling of an eye. To put away the document map and see only the document on-screen, click the Document Map button again.

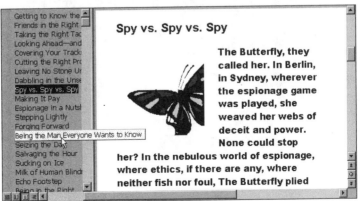

Linking Documents to Save on Work

You can save a lot of time and effort by connecting two documents so that changes made to the first are made automatically to the second. This process is called *linking*. If a table in a memo you are working on happens to be useful in an annual report as well, you can link the documents, and updates to the table in the memo will show up in the annual report as well.

Word offers two kinds of links, automatic and manual:

✦ With an *automatic link*, changes made to the original document are made in the linked document as well each time you reopen the linked document. Text is displayed in full if the link is automatic.

✦ With a *manual link*, you have to tell Word 97 to update the link. Manual links are represented in the text by an icon. The text or graphic in the original file does not appear.

Creating a link

To link documents this way:

1. Open the document with the text you want to link.

2. Select the text and copy it to the Clipboard by clicking the Copy button, pressing Ctrl+C, or choosing Edit⇨Copy.

3. Switch to the document where the linked text is to be pasted and put the cursor where you want the text to go.

4. Choose Edit⇨Paste Special. The Paste Special dialog box appears.

5. Click the Paste Link radio button.

6. If the thing being linked is not text, choose Microsoft Word Document Object, Unformatted Text, or Picture in the As box.

7. To begin with, Word 97 creates an automatic link, but if you want to create a manual link, click Display as Icon. A picture of the Change icon appears in the lower-right corner of the dialog box. This is the icon that appears in the document instead of the linked text or the linked graphic. (Click the Change Icon button if you want to choose an icon of your own for manual links.)

8. Click OK.

This figure shows two links in a document, a manual link and an automatic link. The manual link is represented by a Change icon. When I clicked the automatic link, the text changed to gray to show that it was put here with the Edit⇨Paste Special command.

Manual link   Automatic link

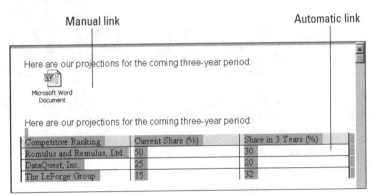

Here are our projections for the coming three-year period:

Microsoft Word
Document

Here are our projections for the coming three-year period:

Competitive Ranking	Current Share (%)	Share in 3 Years (%)
Romulus and Remulus, Ltd.	50	30
DataQuest, Inc.	25	20
The LeForge Group	15	32

TIP

To convert a Change icon into the original text that it represents, select the icon, choose Edit⇨Linked Document Object⇨Convert, click the Display as Icon check box to remove the check mark, and click OK. Do the same to change linked text back into an icon, but put the check mark back in the Display as Icon check box.

Updating, breaking, and changing links

With an automatic link, changes made to the original document are made to the linked document whenever the linked document is reopened. With manual links, however, you have to tell Word 97 to update the link.

To update a link — and do other things besides — go to the Links dialog box:

1. Choose Edit⇨Links.

2. In the Links dialog box, select the link you want to update. Be sure to look at the Source File listing at the bottom of the dialog box to make sure you're updating the right link.

3. Click the Update Now button.

4. Click OK.

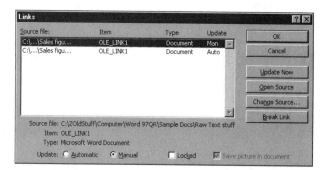

You can update several links at the same time by Ctrl+clicking the links before you click the Update Now button.

The Links dialog box offers several more buttons and check boxes for handling links:

✦ **Open Source:** Opens the original document so that you can make changes to text.

✦ **Change Source:** If you move the original document to another folder, Word 97 doesn't know where to look for the document that contains the original text. Click this button to open the Change Source dialog box. Then find the original document and click Open. The link is re-established.

✦ **Break Link:** Severs the tie between the original document and the document with the link in it. When you click this button, the link is broken and you can't get it back.

✦ **Automatic:** Click this option button to change the link to an automatic link.

✦ **Manual:** Click to change the link to a manual link.

✦ **Locked:** Makes it so that updates to the original document do not affect the linked document. Choose this option instead of

Break Link if you want to break the link but still be able to go to the original document if you have to.

✦ **Save Picture in Document:** Saves the link in your document as a "picture." This option is for use with graphics and is designed to save disk space. Instead of saving the computer code used to create the graphic, Word 97 saves a picture of the graphic.

Suppose you're in the linked document and you realize that you need to change the original text. If the link is a manual one, all you have to do is double-click the Microsoft Word Document icon to get to the original text. With an automatic link, choose Edit⇨Linked Document Object⇨Open Link or right-click and choose Linked Document Object⇨Open Link from the shortcut menu.

To make sure that all links are updated before you print documents, choose Tools⇨Options, click the Print tab, and click the Update Links box.

If you delete the original file, that's the end of your link. You can't get it back. So long, Charlie.

Besides links, you can also create *hyperlinks* — a link between two documents or two different places in the same document. By clicking on a hyperlink, you go directly to the other document or other place in the same document. *See* "Hyperlinking in Word 97" in Part VII to learn how to put a hyperlink in a document.

Master Documents for Really Big Jobs

For really big jobs like books, create a *master document*. A master document is a collection of subdocuments that make up the book. Master documents make it easier to organize and manage big jobs. Every change you make in a subdocument is made to the master document as well, and changes made to the master document are also made to the subdocument. So all you have to do is go to the master document and collapse or expand the headings to see how your work is progressing.

With a master document, it's easy to promote or demote headings. All you have to do is click buttons on the Master Document toolbar. You can also move text easily in a master document. And when you want to see how your book is organized, all you have to do is change to Master Document view and have a look.

If you just started writing and organizing your opus, creating a master document is easy. It's a bit harder to assemble documents you've already written or are working on and put them in a master document.

Master documents and their subdocuments are easier to handle and work with if you save them in one folder.

Creating a new master document

To create a new master document:

1. Click the New button, press Ctrl+N, or choose File➪New to open a new document.

2. Choose View➪Master Document. The Master Document toolbar appears. Many of these tools are the same as those on the Outline toolbar.

3. Enter the chapter titles and headings. This is the outline you will use to write your book. As you enter headings and titles, use the Style drop-down menu to assign heading levels. For example, give the Heading 1 style to chapter titles. Assign headings and sub-headings within chapters styles Heading 2, Heading 3, and so on.

4. Select the first batch of headings to turn them into a subdocument and click the Create Subdocument button.

5. Keep doing this until you've selected and created all the subdocuments. When you're done, your document looks something like the following. Notice the subdocument icons on the left.

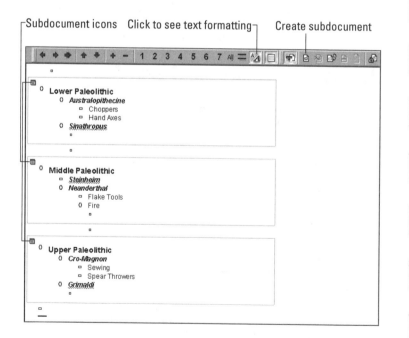

Subdocument icons   Click to see text formatting   Create subdocument

6. Choose File⇨Save to save the master document and all its subdocuments.

7. Choose a folder to save the file in, type a descriptive name for the master document in the File Name box, and click the Save button.

Word 97 creates and names the subdocuments as well as the master document. Word gets subdocument names from the subdocument's first heading.

Assembling documents for a master document

Maybe you've already written several documents and want to assemble them into a master document. Follow these instructions:

1. Click the New button, press Ctrl+N, or choose File⇨New to open a new document.

2. Choose View⇨Master Document.

3. Click the Insert Subdocument button.

4. In the Insert Subdocument dialog box, find and select the first document that you want to include in your master document.

5. Click the Open button. Word inserts the file.

6. If styles in the subdocument and master document conflict, Word 97 asks what to do about it. You can apply the subdocument's styles or use the styles in the master document by clicking Yes or No.

7. Click the 1, 2, or 3 button to see only the first one, two, or three levels of headings. That makes it easier to work in Master Document View.

8. Go to the bottom of the master document, click the Insert Subdocument button, and insert another file. Keep doing this until you've inserted all the subdocuments.

9. Choose File⇨Save As to save the master document and all its subdocuments.

10. Choose a folder to save the master document in, type a descriptive name for the master document in the File name box, and click the Save button.

Working on master documents and subdocuments

After you create the master document and its subdocuments, you can start working on your grand opus. Subdocuments work like ordinary Word documents, but when you open the master document you see, instead of subdocuments, hyperlinks to the subdocuments. Click a hyperlink and the subdocument opens so that you can work on it.

Or, if you want to work inside the master document, click the Expand Subdocuments button. Instead of hyperlinks, you see all the subdocuments. You can still open subdocuments from here. To do so, double-click a subdocument icon.

Removing, moving, locking, splitting, merging, and renaming subdocuments

To remove or rearrange subdocuments, open the master document and change to Master Document view by choosing View⇨Master Document. Click the Expand Subdocuments button and then click the 1 button to see only the first heading in every subdocument. Do the following:

✦ **Removing:** Select the subdocument by clicking its subdocument icon. Then click the Remove Subdocument button or press the Delete key. Removing a subdocument this way does not delete the subdocument — it merely removes it from the master document.

✦ **Moving:** Word 97 says that you can move a subdocument by clicking its icon and dragging its icon to a new place, but when I try to do this I only succeed in dropping one subdocument into another. To move a subdocument, I prefer to remove it and then reinsert it.

✦ **Moving a heading:** Click the icon to the left of the heading and drag it to a new location.

✦ **Merging:** To merge two subdocuments and make them a single subdocument, move the subdocuments so that they are next to each other, if necessary. Select the first by clicking its subdocument icon, and select the second by Shift+clicking its icon. You can merge more than one document by Shift+clicking this way. Finally, click the Merge Subdocument button and save the master document.

✦ **Splitting:** To divide a subdocument in two parts and create two subdocuments, select the heading that you want to be the first in the new subdocument. Do this by clicking its icon. Then click the Split Subdocument button.

✦ **Renaming:** To rename a subdocument, you have to do so within the master document. Click the subdocument icon to open the subdocument. Choose File⇨Save As, type a new name in the File Name text box, and click Save. Then close the subdocument.

✦ **Locking:** If you are sharing your master document with others, you can lock subdocuments to keep others from tampering with them. When a subdocument is locked, people can read it but not change it in any way. To lock a subdocument, click its icon and click the Lock Document button. You'll see the Lock icon below the subdocument icon. Click the Lock Document button again to unlock the subdocument.

Outlines for Organizing Your Work

Outline view is a great way to see at a glance how your document is organized and whether you need to organize it a differently. To take advantage of this feature, you must have used the Style menu to assign heading levels to the headings in your document. In Outline view, you can see all the headings in your document. If a section is in the wrong place, you can move it simply by dragging an icon or by pressing one of the buttons on the Outline toolbar.

To see a document in Outline view, choose View⇨Outline or click the Outline View button in the lower-left corner of the screen. Here is a sample document in Outline view with the All button selected to show all the headings and the normal text in paragraphs.

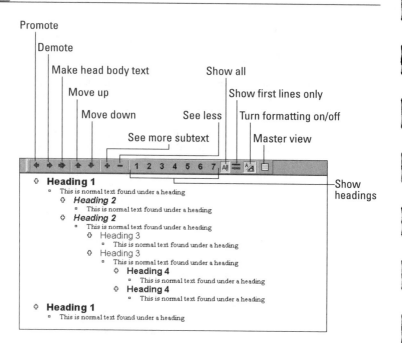

To change how much of a document you see in Outline view:

✦ **Headings:** Click a Show Heading button (1 through 7) to see different heading levels.

✦ **All headings:** Click the All button to see the whole show.

✦ **Headings in one section:** If you want to see the headings and text in only one section of a document, choose that section by clicking the plus sign beside it, and then click the Expand button. Click the Collapse button when you're done.

✦ **Normal text:** Click the Show First Line Only button to see only the first line in each paragraph. First lines are followed by an ellipsis (...) so you know that more text follows.

Notice the plus icons and square icons next to the headings and the text. A plus icon means that the heading has subtext under it. For example, headings almost always have plus icons because text comes after them, but body text has a square icon because it is lowest on the Outline totem pole.

To select text in Outline view, click either the plus sign or the square icon. To select more than one section, Shift+click its icon. After the text has been selected, you can do the following tasks:

✦ **Promote a head:** Click the Promote button to move a heading up the ladder. For example, you can promote a Heading 2 to a Heading 1.

✦ **Demote a head:** Click the Demote button to bust down a Heading 1 to a Heading 2, for example. When you promote or demote a head or section, you do the same to all the subtext beneath it.

✦ **Make a head into normal text:** Click the Demote to Body Text button to make a heading into text.

✦ **Move a section:** To move a section up or down in the document, click the Move Up or Move Down button. You can also drag the plus sign or square icon to a new location. If you want to move the subordinate text and headings along with the section, click the Collapse button to tuck all the subtext into the heading before you move it.

Rearranging the Toolbars

To make it easier to work with toolbars, you can drag them around on-screen. You can remove buttons from the toolbars and replace them with buttons of your own choosing. You can also create your own toolbars and even invent new toolbar buttons.

To find out what a button on a toolbar does, move the mouse pointer over it. A one- or two-word description appears. If you're not seeing the descriptions, choose Tools➪Customize, click the Options tab of the Customize dialog box, and click the Show ScreenTips on toolbars check box.

Displaying other toolbars

Two toolbars appear at the top of the Word 97 window: the Standard toolbar and the Formatting toolbar. To place new toolbars in the window, right-click on a toolbar (but not on one of its buttons) and click the toolbar's name on the shortcut menu.

You can also choose View➪Toolbars and click a name on the submenu. What's more, you can display the Web toolbar and Drawing toolbar by clicking their buttons on the Standard toolbar.

After a toolbar is on-screen, try dragging it into the window and repositioning it or changing its shape:

✦ To reposition a toolbar, click the toolbar (but not on a button) and drag it into the window.

✦ To change a toolbar's shape, place the mouse on a border. When you see the two-headed arrow, drag the border until the toolbar is the shape you want.

This figure shows all the Word 97 toolbars on the shortcut menu. They have been dragged into the window and reshaped.

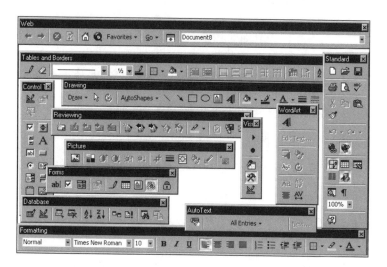

TIP To remove a toolbar you've dragged into the window, click its Close button (the *X* in the upper-right corner). Double-click its title bar to move it back to its rightful place at the top or bottom of the window.

Putting your own buttons on toolbars

For all I know, you never do some of the tasks that the buttons on the Standard and Formatting toolbars were put there to help you do. If you're not using a button, you can take it off the toolbar and replace it with a button you do use. Adding buttons to and removing buttons from toolbars is easy, and if you make a mistake, it's easy to get the original toolbars back. If you don't have Microsoft Excel, for example, you can chuck the Insert Microsoft Excel Worksheet button and put a button you do use in its place.

To decide for yourself which buttons appear on toolbars:

1. Put the toolbar whose buttons you want to change on-screen.

2. Choose Tools➪Customize, or right-click a toolbar and choose Customize from the shortcut menu. The Customize dialog box appears.

The Categories list in this dialog box lists all the toolbars and menus in Word 97 along with the styles, macros, AutoText entries, and fonts that are available in the template you're using. If you aren't sure what a button does, click it in the Commands box and then click the Description button.

3. Remove or add a button from a toolbar. To do so, you leave the Customize dialog box and click on the toolbars on the screen:

- **Removing:** To remove a button from a toolbar, simply drag it off the toolbar. As you drag, a gray rectangle appears above the pointer and an *X* appears below it. Release the mouse button and the toolbar button disappears.

- **Adding:** To add a button, click in the Categories box on the toolbar or menu whose button you want to add. Then, in the Commands box, click on the button. Gently drag the button out of the Customize dialog box and place it on the toolbar where you want it to appear. As you do so, a gray rectangle appears above the cursor and a plus sign appears below it.

4. If you want your new toolbar arrangement to appear only in certain templates, click the Save In drop-down menu and choose the template.

5. Click Close.

You can also move buttons between toolbars by dragging them from toolbar to toolbar while the Customize dialog box is open.

If you make a boo-boo and wish that you hadn't fooled with the buttons on the toolbar, choose Tools➪Customize or right-click a toolbar and choose Customize to get to the Customize dialog box.

From there, click the Toolbars tab, click on the toolbar whose buttons you fooled with, and click the Reset button. Click OK in the Reset Toolbar dialog box.

Creating your own toolbar

You can also create a new toolbar with your favorite buttons on it. If you want, you can even create toolbar buttons for styles, fonts, AutoText entries, and macros.

1. Choose Tools⇨Customize, or right-click a toolbar and choose Customize from the shortcut menu to see the Customize dialog box.

2. Click the Toolbars tab.

3. Click the New button. The New Toolbar dialog box appears:

```
┌─────────────────────────────────────┐
│ New Toolbar                    ? X   │
│ Toolbar name:                        │
│ ┌─────────────────────────────────┐ │
│ │ My Favorite Buttons             │ │
│ └─────────────────────────────────┘ │
│ Make toolbar available to:           │
│ ┌───────────────────────────────┬─┐ │
│ │ Normal.dot                    │▼│ │
│ └───────────────────────────────┴─┘ │
│          ┌──────┐   ┌────────┐       │
│          │  OK  │   │ Cancel │       │
│          └──────┘   └────────┘       │
└─────────────────────────────────────┘
```

4. Type a name for your toolbar in the Toolbar Name box. The name you type here will appear on the View⇨Toolbars submenu.

5. If necessary, choose a template in the Make Toolbar Available to drop-down list.

6. Click OK. A tiny toolbar with the name you entered appears on the screen.

7. Double-click the title bar of your new toolbar to move it to the top of the screen.

8. Click the Commands tab in the Customize dialog box.

9. In the Categories box, click on the menu or toolbar whose commands you want to include in your new toolbar. You will find macros, fonts, AutoText entries, and styles at the bottom of the Categories menu.

10. To add a button, click it in the Commands box and drag it right onto your new toolbar. Drag as many buttons onto the toolbar as you need. For now, don't worry about their position on the toolbar. Simply drag them onto the left side, to the first position.

11. When you've added all the buttons, drag them where you want them to stand on the toolbar.

12. If you've added styles or fonts, you might want to shorten their names to make them fit better on the toolbar. To do that, right-click on the button whose name you want to shorten and enter a new name in the Name text box. Also on the shortcut menu are commands for changing buttons' appearances.

13. When your toolbar is just-so, click Close.

Here is a toolbar I created myself. Instead of choosing these styles from the Style drop-down menu, all I have to do is click a button on this toolbar:

 You can always delete a toolbar you made yourself. Choose Tools⇨Customize or right-click a toolbar and choose Customize to get to the Customize dialog box. Then click the Toolbars tab, click on the toolbar you want to extinguish, and click the Delete button. Click OK when Word asks if you really want to go through with it.

Repeating an Action — and Quicker This Time

 The Edit menu has a command called Repeat that you can choose to repeat your last action, and it can be a mighty time-saver. The command changes names, depending on what you did last.

For example, if you just changed a heading style, the command is called Edit⇨Repeat Style. To change another heading in the same way, move the cursor to the heading and choose Edit⇨Repeat Style (or press F4 or Ctrl+Y) instead of going to the trouble of clicking the Style menu and choosing a heading style from the drop-down list.

If you had to type "I will not talk in class" a hundred times, all you would have to do is write it once and choose Edit⇨Repeat Typing (or press F4 or Ctrl+Y) 99 times.

Similar to the Edit⇨Repeat command is the Redo button. It "redoes" the commands you "undid" with the Undo menu or Undo button. If you've "undone" a bunch of commands and regret having done so, pull down the Redo menu by clicking its down arrow and choose the commands you thoughtlessly "undid" the first time around.

Searching with Wildcards

When you can't find a file or are searching for a word in a document, wildcards can come in handy. A *wildcard* is a single character or group of characters that represent characters in a filename or word. This table lists common wildcards and explains how to use them.

Wildcard	How to Use It
?	Represents a single character. Entering **Peter?.doc** in a Find File dialog box finds files named *Peter1.doc* and *Peter2.doc,* but not *Peter10.doc.*
*	Represents a group of characters or a single character. Entering **Peter*.doc** finds *Peter1.doc* as well as *Peter10.doc.*
[xx]	Represents specific characters to search for, where *xx* are the characters. Entering **P[ae]ter.doc** finds files named *Pater.doc* and *Peter.doc,* but not *Piter.doc* or *Puter.doc.*
[!x]	Represents a character you *don't* want to find, where *x* is the character. Entering **P[!e]ter.doc** finds *Pater.doc, Piter.doc,* and *Poter.doc,* but not *Peter.doc.*
[x-z]	Represents a group of consecutive characters, where *x* and *z* are the characters. Entering **P[b-d]ter.doc** finds *Pbter.doc, Pcter.doc,* and *Pdter.doc,* but not *Pater.doc* or *Peter.doc.*

Desktop Publishing

Once upon a time, word processors were nothing more than glorified typewriters. They were good for typing and basic formatting, but not much else. Over the years, however, Microsoft Word and other word processors have become desktop publishing applications in their own right.

Part VI explains advanced formatting techniques in Word 97. If you're in charge of the company newsletter, or you just want to impress your impressionable friends, check out the entries in this part.

In this part . . .

✔ **Keeping text and graphics in the same place**

✔ **Putting borders and shading on pages, graphics, and text boxes**

✔ **Changing the color of text**

✔ **Creating, editing, and formatting tables**

✔ **Positioning text boxes and graphics**

✔ **Creating "landscape" documents**

✔ **Importing clip art into a document**

Anchoring Text and Graphics

Suppose you want a paragraph or a graphic to stay in the same place. Normally, what is in the middle of page 1 is pushed to the bottom of the page or to page 2 when you insert paragraphs at the start of a document. What if you want the paragraph or graphic to stay put, come hell or high water?

In that case, you can *anchor* it to the page. After you drop anchor, text flows around your graphic or paragraph, and your graphic or paragraph stays put.

The following steps explain how to anchor text or a graphic to a page. To anchor text, place it in a text box first (*see* "Working with Text Boxes" at the end of this part if you need help with that). You're all set to go if you are anchoring a graphic.

1. Switch to Page Layout view if you are not already there by clicking the Page Layout View button in the lower-left corner of the screen.

2. Click the Zoom Control drop-down menu on the Standard toolbar and choose 50%. It helps to get a bird's-eye view of a document when you are laying it out.

3. Click inside the text box or graphic to select it. If you do this correctly, selection handles (small squares) appear on the corners and sides of the thing you clicked on.

4. Choose Format➪Text Box if you are anchoring a text box or Format➪Picture if you are anchoring a graphic image. You see the Format Text Box or the Format Picture dialog box.

5. Click the Position tab.

6. Click the <u>L</u>ock Anchor check box.

7. Click the <u>M</u>ove Object with Text check box to remove the check mark. As soon as you do so, the <u>V</u>ertical <u>F</u>rom setting changes to Page.

8. In the <u>H</u>orizontal <u>F</u>rom drop-down menu, choose Page. Now the text box or graphic is locked, horizontally and vertically, to the page, and Word 97 knows to keep it at its current position on the page and *not* move it in the document when text is inserted before it. For now, don't worry about the <u>H</u>orizontal and <u>V</u>ertical settings. In step 10 you will drag the text box or graphic on the page exactly where you want it to be. Placing the text object or graphic by entering numbers in the <u>H</u>orizontal and <u>V</u>ertical boxes isn't worth the hassle.

9. Click OK in the Format dialog box. Back in your document, the text box or graphic is no doubt in the wrong place.

10. Slide the pointer over the border of the graphic frame or text box. When you see a four-headed cross, click and drag the text box or graphic where you want it to stay put on the page.

The following figure shows an example of an anchored text box and graphic. No matter how much news goes before this anchored text box, this important notice stays on the side of page 1 where all can see it.

To tell if a text box or graphic has been locked, click the Show/Hide ¶ button and look for the picture of an anchor and a padlock in the left margin of the document.

See also "Wrapping Text around a Text Box or Graphic," later in this part, to tell Word what nearby text should do when it bumps up against a text box or graphic.

Bordering, Shading, and Coloring Backgrounds for Text

By placing borders around text and shading the area inside the borders or filling it with color, you can brighten up a page considerably. Here is an example of an announcement that has been shaded and given a "shadow" border:

> The building manager and the fire department will conduct a test of the fire alarms in the building on Tuesday, September 26 at 10:00. Ignore the fire alarms—unless, of course, there is a real fire.

If you want to be able to move the text on the page after you have formatted it, put it in a text box first. *See also* "Working with Text Boxes," later in this part to learn how to do that. *See also* "Putting Borders and Color Shades on Text Boxes and Graphics," also in this part, to learn the secrets of putting borders on text boxes.

The fastest but crudest way to put borders around paragraphs is to select the paragraphs and click the Outside Border button. To put a borderline along the top, bottom, or sides of text, click the drop-down menu beside the Outside Border button and choose a border.

Besides the generic borders you get with the Outside Border button, you can choose borders of different widths and shade the area within the borders as well. Here's how:

1. Select the paragraph or paragraphs to which you want to add borders and shading.

2. Choose Format➪Borders and Shading. The Borders tab of the Borders and Shading dialog box appears:

Borders and Shading `? X`

Borders | Page Border | Shading

Setting:

None

Box

Shadow

Three-D

Custom

Style:

Color:

Auto

Width:

4 ½ pt

Preview

Click on diagram below or use buttons to apply borders

Apply to:

Paragraph

Options...

Show Toolbar

OK | Cancel

3. Under Setting, choose which kind of border you want. If you want to put borders around one, two, or three sides of the paragraph or paragraphs, click the Custom box. Use the None setting to remove borders.

4. Under Style, scroll down the list and choose a line for the borders. You will find interesting choices at the bottom of the menu. Be sure to look in the Preview window to see what your choices in this dialog box add up to.

5. Click the Color drop-down menu and choose a color for the borderlines, if you so desire and if you have a color printer.

6. The Width drop-down menu is where you decide how wide the lines you chose for the borders are. Make a choice from the drop-down menu.

7. The four buttons in the Preview window are for telling Word which sides of the paragraphs are to have borders. Click these buttons to remove or add borders as you wish.

8. Click the Options button and fill in the Border and Shading Options dialog box if you want to get specific about how close the text can come to the borders.

9. Either click OK to apply the borders you so carefully constructed or click the Shading tab (and read on) to shade the text as well as put borders around it.

Do the following to shade or put a color background behind a paragraph or paragraphs:

1. If the Borders and Shading dialog box is not already open, select the text and choose Format➪Borders and Shading. Then click the Shading tab.

2. Either shade the text or give it a color background:

- To shade text, click one of the gray boxes under Fill or click the down-arrow in the Style box and choose a gray pattern from the drop-down menu. You will find interesting and bizarre patterns at the bottom of the menu. Click None or choose the Clear style to remove shading.

- To put a color background behind text, click a color or choose one from the Color menu.

3. Click OK.

If you're in a hurry, you can also border, shade, and color text with the Tables and Borders toolbar:

1. Select the text you want to gussy up.

2. Right-click on a toolbar and choose Tables and Borders.

3. From the Line Style menu, choose a line.

4. Click the down-arrow on the Line Weight menu and choose a line thickness.

5. To make the border line a color or gray shade, click the Border Color button and make a choice.

6. Click the Border down-arrow and make choices from the drop-down menu if you want to put borders on specific parts of the text.

7. To shade the text or give it a background color, click the Shading Color down-arrow and click on a color or shade.

Borders and Color Shades for Graphics and Text Boxes

By playing with the borders around graphics and text boxes and by putting interesting gray shades and colors behind text and images, you can amuse yourself on a rainy afternoon. And you can sometimes create fanciful artwork. These text boxes and graphics were created by a seven-year-old with help from his father. This part of the book explains how to put borders and gray shades like these on graphics and text boxes.

Putting borders on text boxes and graphics

The fastest way to put a border around a graphic, text box, or AutoShape is to select it, click the Line Style button on the Picture or Drawing toolbar, and choose a line. To see the Picture or Drawing toolbar, right-click on any toolbar and choose Drawing or Picture from the shortcut menu.

To get fancy with borders, click the graphic, text box, or AutoShape to which you want to give borders and do the following:

1. Choose Format and then choose the bottom-most command on the Format menu. Which command that is — Picture, Object, Text Box, or AutoShape — depends on what kind of object you are working on.

2. Click the Colors and Lines tab in the Format dialog box.

3. Under Line, click the Color drop-down menu and choose a color (Black is the first choice in the box). Click the No Line option to remove borders from an object.

4. Click the Dashed down arrow and choose a dashed or dotted line, if you want.

5. Click the Style down arrow and tell Word what kind of line you want. You will find exotic choices at the bottom of the menu.

6. Click arrows in the Weight box or enter a number yourself to tell Word how wide or narrow to make the borderlines.

7. Click OK.

Filling a text box or graphic with a color or gray shade

The fast way to "fill" a graphic or text box is to select it, click the down arrow beside the Fill Color button on the Drawing toolbar, and choose a color or gray shade. By clicking Fill Effects at the bottom of the menu, you can get to interesting gray shades and textures.

Or, if you are the kind who likes dialog boxes, select the thing you are "filling," choose Format, and then choose the bottom-most command on the Format menu — Picture, Object, Text Box, or AutoShape. Then click the Colors and Shapes tab in the Format dialog box, click the Color drop-down menu, and make a choice.

Coloring Text

If you're lucky enough to own or have access to a color printer, you can print text in different colors. And even if you don't own a color printer, you can change the color of text on-screen. You might do that to call attention to parts of a document, for example. Word 97 offers 14 colors, plus white, black, and two gray shades. Besides coloring the letters themselves, you can color the space between the letters.

To change the color of text, follow these steps:

1. Select the text.

2. Click the down arrow beside the Font Color button and click on a color, on black, on white, or on one of the two gray shades.

You can get the same color choices on the Color menu in the Font dialog box. To get there, choose Format⇨Font.

To remove the color from text, select it, click the Font Color drop-down menu, and choose Automatic.

See also "Borders and Color Shades for Graphics and Text Boxes," to see how to put a color background behind text.

Constructing the Perfect Table

As everyone who has ever worked on one knows, tables are a chore. Getting all the columns to fit, making columns and rows the right width and height, and editing the text in a table is not easy. So problematic are tables that Word 97 has devoted an entire menu to constructing them: the T̲able menu. Fortunately for you, the commands on this menu make formatting and working with tables easy.

This section explains how to create tables, enter text into tables, change the number and size of columns and rows, sort tables, and format tables.

Like so much else in Computerland, tables have their own jargon. A *cell* is the box that is formed where a row and column intersect. Each cell holds one data item. The *header row* is the name of the labels along the top row that explain what is in the columns below. *Borders* are the lines in the table. The *gridlines* are the gray lines that show where the columns and rows are. Gridlines are not printed — they appear to help you format your table. Word prints only the borders when you print a table.

	Wins	Losses	Ties	Goals Scored	Goals Scored On	Shots On Goal
Spiders	7	1	0	49	5	103
Knights	5	2	1	15	12	45
Bandits	4	2	2	9	14	39
River Kings	3	4	1	8	19	18
Bears	1	7	0	3	31	14

Borders — Header row — Cells — Column — Row

Thanks everybody for a great football season!

If you are having a lot of trouble making a table fit on the page, try printing it as a landscape document. *See also* "Landscape Documents," later in this part.

The best way to work on tables is in Page Layout view. You need to see precisely how wide the columns are and where they fall on the page. If you're a fan of Normal view, however, make sure the wrap to window feature is turned off when you construct tables. To turn it off, choose T̲ools➪O̲ptions, click the View tab, and click to remove the check mark from the W̲rap to Window check box.

Creating a table

Word 97 offers no less than four ways to create the cells and rows for a table: the Insert Table button, the Draw Table button, the Table⇨Insert Table command, and the Table⇨Convert Text to Table command.

The fastest way to create a table is to click the Insert Table button on the Standard toolbar:

1. Place the cursor where you want the table to go.

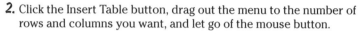

2. Click the Insert Table button, drag out the menu to the number of rows and columns you want, and let go of the mouse button.

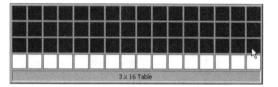

3 x 16 Table

That's easy enough. Another easy way is to make like your computer is a scratch pad and draw a table. This is the best way to create a table because you can get rows and columns of different widths and heights. As "Merging and splitting cells and tables," a bit later in this part explains, getting "merged" and "split" cells with the commands on the Table menu is far more difficult than simply drawing merged and split cells. To draw a table:

1. Right-click and choose Draw Table from the shortcut menu.

2. Start drawing the table. As you drag the pencil on-screen, you get columns and rows.

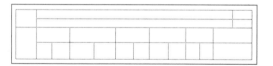

3. If you make a mistake, click the Eraser button on the Tables and Border toolbar (it appeared on screen when you chose Draw Table from the shortcut menu). The pointer changes into an eraser. Drag it over the parts of the table you regret drawing.

4. When you've finished drawing your table, click the Draw Table button to put the pencil away safely for use another day.

The only advantage of the Table⇨Insert Table command is that it gives you a chance to choose one of Word's formats for your table:

1. Place the cursor where you want the table to be.

2. Choose Table⇨Insert Table. The Insert Table dialog box appears.

3. In the Number of Columns box, enter the number of columns you want.

4. In the Number of Rows box, enter the number of rows you want.

5. Word 97 gives columns a uniform width based on how many columns are in the table and how wide the margins are, but you can change the width of all columns in the table by clicking the arrows in the Column width box.

6. Click the AutoFormat button to open a dialog box from which you can choose one of Word 97's table formats. These formats are explained in the section "Formatting a table with Word's 'AutoFormats'."

7. Click OK.

The fourth way to create a table is to convert text that you've already entered. This is the way to go if you've created a list and you don't want to go to the trouble of re-entering the text all over again for the new table. To convert text into a table:

1. Press Tab in the list where you want columns to be divided. For example, if you are turning an address list into a table, put all the names and addresses on one line and press Tab after the first name, the last name, the street address, the city, the state, and the zip code. For this to work, each name and address — each line — must have the same number of tabs in it.

2. Start a new paragraph — press Enter, that is — where you want each row to end.

3. Select the text you want to turn into a table.

4. Choose Table⇨Convert Text to Table.

5. Under Separate text at in the Convert Text to Table dialog box, choose Tabs to tell Word 97 how the columns are separated.

6. Click OK.

In this illustration, five tab stops were entered on each line in an address list (I've clicked the Show/Hide¶ button so that you can see where Tab was pressed). Below the list is the table that was created from the address list.

```
Roger Wilco    →  1227 Jersey St. →San Francisco  →  CA  →  94114→415/555-1234¶
Bert Tangent   →  3349 Pax St.  →  Pacifica→CA  →  94404→415/555-4321¶
J.S. Min→910 Jay St.   →   Daly City   →   CA  →  94404→415/555-1423¶
```

Roger Wilco	1227 Jersey St.	San Francisco	CA	94114	415/555-1234
Bert Tangent	3349 Pax St.	Pacific	CA	94404	415/555-4321
J.S. Min	910 Jay St.	Daly City	CA	94404	415/555-1423

Entering text and numbers in a table

After you've created the table and can see the gridlines (the gray lines that divide the rows and columns), you can start entering text. (If you don't see the gridlines, or if you don't want to see them for that matter, choose Table⇨Show Gridlines.) All you have to do is click in a cell and start typing. To help you work more quickly, here are some shortcuts for moving the cursor in a table:

Press	Moves the Cursor to
Tab	Next column in row
Shift+Tab	Previous column in row
Alt+Home	Start of row
Alt+End	End of row
↓	Row below
↑	Row above
Alt+Page Up	Top of column
Alt+Page Down	Bottom of column

If you need to add a row at the bottom of the table to enter more text, place the cursor in the last column of the last row and press the Tab key.

Changing the layout of a table

Very likely, you created too many or too few rows or columns for your table. Some columns are probably too wide, and others may be too narrow. If that is the case, you have to change the layout of the table by deleting, inserting, and changing the size of columns and rows. (Putting borders around tables and embellishing them in other ways is explained later in this entry.)

This section explains

+ Selecting rows, columns, and an entire table

+ Inserting and deleting columns and rows

+ Rearranging columns and rows

+ Resizing columns and rows

Before you can fool with cells, rows, or columns, you have to select them:

+ **Cells:** To select a cell, click in it. You can select several cells at once by dragging the cursor over them.

+ **Rows:** Place the cursor in the left margin and click to select one row, or click and drag to select several. You can also select rows by placing the cursor in the row you want to select and then choosing the Table⇨Select Row command. To select several rows, select cells in the rows and then choose Table⇨Select Row.

+ **Columns:** To select a column, move the cursor to the top of the column. When the cursor changes into a fat down-pointing arrow, click once. You can click and drag to select several columns. The other way to select a column is to click anywhere in the column and choose Table⇨Select Column. To select several columns with this command, select cells in the columns and then choose Table⇨Select Column.

+ **A table:** To select a table, click in the table and choose Table⇨Select Table or press Alt+5 (the 5 on the numeric keypad, not the one on the keyboard).

Here's the lowdown on inserting and deleting columns and rows:

+ **Inserting columns:** To insert a blank column, select the column to the right of where you want the new column to go. If you want to insert two or more columns, select the number of columns you want to add. Then choose Table⇨Insert Columns, right-click in the selection and choose Insert Columns from the shortcut menu, or simply press the Insert Table button on the Standard toolbar (now it's called Insert Columns).

+ **Deleting columns:** To delete columns, select them. Then either choose Table⇨Delete Columns or right-click the selection and choose Delete Columns.

+ **Inserting rows:** To insert a blank row, select the row below which you want the new one to appear. If you want to insert more than one row, select more than one. Then choose Table⇨Insert Rows, right-click in the selection and choose Insert Rows from the shortcut menu, or just press the Insert Table button on the toolbar (it's called Insert Rows now). You can also insert a row at the end of a table by moving the cursor into the last cell in the last row and pressing Tab.

+ **Deleting rows:** To delete rows, select them and choose Table⇨Delete Rows, or else right-click and choose Delete Rows from the shortcut menu.

Because there is no elegant way to move a column or row, you should move only one at a time. If you try to move several at once, you open a can of worms that is best left unopened. To move a column or row:

1. Select the column or row you want to move.

2. Right-click in the selection and choose Cut from the shortcut menu. The column or row disappears to the Clipboard.

3. Move the column or row:

- **Column:** Move the cursor across the top of the columns and slide it delicately to the spot between two existing columns to which you want to move the column. When the cursor turns into a fat down-pointing arrow, right-click and choose Paste Columns from the shortcut menu.

- **Row:** Move the cursor into the first column of the row below which you want to move your row. In other words, if you're placing the row between what are now rows 6 and 7, put the cursor in row 7. Then right-click and choose Paste Rows from the shortcut menu.

By far, the easiest way to change the width of columns and the height of rows is to "eyeball it." To make a column wider or narrower, simply move the cursor onto a gridline. When the cursor changes into what looks like a German cross, start dragging. Tug and pull, tug and pull until the column looks just right. You can also slide the column bars on the ruler (if you're in Page Layout view) to change the width of columns. When you move the pointer over a column bar, the words "Move Table Column" appear.

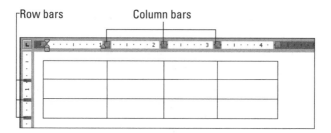

Word 97 adjusts the height of rows to accommodate text, but you can change row heights yourself by dragging the row bars on the vertical ruler (in Page Layout view). When you move the pointer over a row bar, you see the words "Adjust Table Row."

The other technique for adjusting row heights and columns widths is to use the Table⇨Cell Height and Width command and blindly try your luck with the settings in the Cell Height and Width dialog box.

This technique isn't nearly as useful as "eyeballing it," however, because the dialog box doesn't have a Preview screen and you can't see what your choices do to the table.

TIP

The Row tab in the Cell Height and Width dialog box is useful for fixing rows that are packed too tightly. To provide more space between rows:

1. Click in the table or, if you want to adjust a few rows, select them.

2. Choose Table⇨Cell Height and Width.

3. In the Height of Rows menu, choose At Least to make sure that there is a certain minimum amount of space between rows. If you want all the rows to be the exact same height, choose Exactly. At minimum, rows should be at least 2 points higher than the font you're using. For example, if your letters are 12 points high, your rows should be 14 points high. With the Auto choice, Word makes all the cells in the row the same height as the tallest cell.

4. In the At box, click the arrows to adjust the height of rows. If you chose At Least in step 3, a number already appears in the box. Click the up arrow to add more space between rows.

5. Click OK.

Besides choosing the Auto option to get rows of the same height, you can select the rows and click the Distribute Rows Evenly button on the Tables and Borders toolbar.

The Column tab of the Cell Height and Width dialog box has one useful button called AutoFit. Click it if you've pulled and tugged your columns all out of proportion and want Word 97 to resize columns so that each column is wide enough to contain its widest cell entry. To get columns of uniform width, select them and click the Distribute Columns Evenly button.

Aligning text in columns and rows

To align text in the columns or cells of a table, you can rely on the Align Left, Center, Align Right, and Justify buttons on the Standard toolbar. Select a cell, a column, or columns and click one of these buttons to align the text in a column the same way.

Aligning text across rows, however, is more problematic, especially when the text in the table cells is a different point size, so Word offers three buttons on the Tables and Borders toolbar for aligning text in rows — Align Top, Center Vertically, and Align Bottom. This figure shows how the three buttons align text in rows:

Align Top	Lines up text along the top of each cell in the row.	Text lines up neatly across the top of this row.	
Center Vertically	Lines up text across the middle of each cell in the row.	The text in this row falls straight across the middle.	
Align Bottom	Lines up text along the bottom of each cell in the row.	Text hugs the bottom of this row.	

To align the text across a row in a table, select it, right-click on a toolbar, and choose Tables and Borders from the shortcut menu. Then click one of the align buttons on the toolbar.

Sorting, or reordering, a table

The fastest way to rearrange the rows in a table is to use the Table⇨Sort command or click one of the Sort buttons on the Tables and Borders toolbar. *Sorting* means to rearrange all the rows in a table on the basis of data in one column. For example, the first table shown here is arranged, or sorted, on the fifth column, "Total Votes." This column has been sorted in descending order from most to fewest votes. The second table has been sorted on the first column. It is sorted by the candidates' names in ascending order. Both tables present the same information, but the information has been sorted in different ways.

The difference between ascending and descending sorts is as follows:

✦ Ascending arranges text from A to Z, numbers from smallest to largest, and dates from the oldest in time to the most recent.

✦ Descending arranges text from Z to A, numbers from largest to smallest, and dates from most recent to the oldest in time.

	1st Ward	2nd Ward	3rd Ward	Total Votes
Muñoz	2,567	7,399	10,420	20,386
Wilson	3,113	9,907	4,872	17,892
Teel	67	211	89	367
Greenstein	12	2	113	127

	1st Ward	2nd Ward	3rd Ward	Total Votes
Greenstein	12	2	113	127
Muñoz	2,567	7,399	10,420	20,386
Teel	67	211	89	367
Wilson	3,113	9,907	4,872	17,892

When you rearrange a table by sorting it, Word rearranges the formatting as well as the data. Do your sorting before you format the table.

For simple sorts, select the column that is to be the basis of the sort and click the Sort Descending button for a descending sort or the Sort Ascending button for an ascending sort.

What happens, however, if two people in the table have the same last name and you sort on the last name column? To make sure the table is in alphabetical order, you would have to sort on the first name as well as the last name column to make sure that Wong, David appears before Wong, Winston, for example. For complex sorts like these that involve more than one column, use the Table⇨Sort command.

1. Click in the column that is to be the primary basis of the sort. For example, if you are sorting by last name, click the Last Name column.

2. Choose Table⇨Sort. The Sort dialog box appears:

Sort

Sort by: Last Name — Type: Text — ● Ascending ○ Descending

Then by: First Name — Type: Text — ● Ascending ○ Descending

Then by: Middle Initial — Type: Text — ● Ascending ○ Descending

My list has: ● Header row ○ No header row

OK — Cancel — Options...

3. In the Sort by drop-down list, choose which column to sort the table by.

4. In the Type box, choose Text, Number, or Date if Word 97 hasn't already made the correct choice about what kind of data is in the column you clicked on in step 1.

5. Click the Ascending or Descending option button.

6. The Then By boxes and option buttons work like the Sort By boxes and option buttons, only they are used for breaking ties. In the Sort By dialog box shown here, you can see how the Then By boxes are filled in to make sure that the names in a table are listed in alphabetical order.

7. If your table has a header row, the Header Row option button should already be selected to keep the column labels from getting mixed into the sort. If your table doesn't have a header row, choose the No Header Row option because you want the first row to be rearranged, too. Make sure that these option buttons are chosen correctly.

8. Click OK to sort the table.

Formatting a table with Word's "AutoFormats"

After you enter the text, put the rows and columns in place, and make them the right size, the fun begins. Now you can dress up your table and make it look snazzy.

Almost everything you can do to a document you can do to a table by selecting parts of it and choosing menu commands or clicking buttons. You can change text fonts, align data in the cells in different ways, and even import a graphic into a cell. You can also play with the borders that divide the rows and columns and "shade" columns, rows, and cells by filling them with gray shades or a black background.

The fastest way to get a good-looking table is to let Word 97 do the work for you:

1. Click your table.

2. Choose Table⇨Table AutoFormat. The Table AutoFormat dialog box appears:

Watch this box!

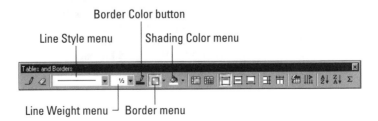

3. Rummage through the Forma<u>t</u>s menu until you find a table to your liking. You can see what tables look like in the Preview box.

4. Check and uncheck the Formats to Apply and Apply Special Formats To check boxes. As you do so, watch the Preview box to see what your choices do.

5. When you have the right table format, click OK.

Getting your own borders, shading, and color

Instead of relying on Word's T<u>a</u>ble⊅Table Auto<u>F</u>ormat command, you can draw borders yourself and shade or give color to different parts of a table as well. Doing so is easier than you might think.

Word 97 has a special toolbar for handling borders, shading, and color in tables. To see it, right-click a toolbar and choose Tables and Borders from the shortcut menu to display the Tables and Borders toolbar. You can also display this toolbar by choosing <u>V</u>iew⊅<u>T</u>oolbars⊅Tables and Borders.

Border Color button

Line Style menu   Shading Color menu

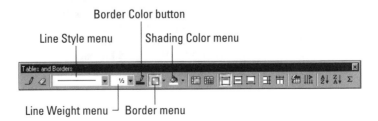

Line Weight menu — Border menu

To put your own borders on a table:

1. Select the part of the table to which you want to apply the border. For example, to put a border on the left side of a cell, select the cell; along the top or bottom of a row, select the row; along the side of a column, select the column; or around an entire table, select it.

2. Click the down arrow beside the Line Style button and choose a line, dashed line, double line, or wiggley line for the border. Choose No Border if you don't want a border or you are removing one that is already there.

3. Click the down arrow beside the Line Weight button to choose a line width for the border.

4. To give the borders a color or gray shade, click the Border Color button and click on one of the boxes that appear. Use the Automatic choice to remove colors and gray shades.

5. Click the down arrow beside the Border button and choose one of the nine border buttons on the menu (use the tenth button, No Border, to remove borders). For example, click the Top Border button to put a border along the top of the part of the table you selected in step 1; click the Inside Border button to put the border on the interior lines of the part of the table you selected.

6. Apply borders to other parts of the table that you selected in step 1:

   - **Same border:** To apply a border of the same line style and weight to another side of the part of the table that you selected in step 1, simply pull down the Border drop-down menu again and click another button.

   - **Different border:** To apply a different border to another side of the part of the table, make choices from the Line Style and Line Weight menus and click a different border button.

7. Select a different part of the table and repeat steps 2 through 6.

Shading, black backgrounds, and color call readers' attention to the important parts of a table. Usually, shading is used in the header row and the summary row — for example, in the "totals" column on the right side of the table or in the bottom row. In this table, the header row has a black background, the highest production figure in each category is shaded at 20% gray, and the Totals row at the bottom is shaded at 40% gray:

Production Plant	Bubble Gum (tons)	Candy Canes (units)	Cotton Candy (acres)	Licorice (sticks)	Lollipops (units)
Boca Raton, FL	119	46,223	918	511,112	290,412
Peoria, IL	335	39,918	456	37,801	871,932
Poughkeepsie, NY	211	118,561	712	567,912	317,206
Waukegan, IL	56	99,987	498	998,912	298,118
Totals	721	304,689	2,584	2,115,737	1,777,668

To "shade" or give a color background to a part of a table:

1. If it's not already on-screen, right-click a toolbar and choose Tables and Borders from the shortcut menu to display the Tables and Borders toolbar.

2. Select the part of the table to which you want to apply the shading or color.

3. Click the down arrow on the Shading Color menu and click one of the buttons.

Repeating header rows on subsequent pages

Making sure that the header row appears on a new page if the table breaks across pages is absolutely essential. Without a header row, readers can't tell what the information in a table is or means. To make the header row (or rows) repeat on the top of each new page, place the cursor in the header row (or select the header rows if you have more than one) and choose Table➪Headings.

Merging and splitting cells and tables

The cells in the first header row of the following table have been merged to create "supercategories." Instead of eight cells, the first row has only four:

West		Midwest		South		East	
California	Washington	Illinois	Nebraska	Georgia	Louisiana	Massachusetts	New York

To merge cells in a table:

1. Select the cells you want to merge.

2. Choose Table➪Merge Cells or click the Merge Cells button on the Tables and Borders toolbar.

In the same vein, you can split a cell into two or more cells:

1. Click in the cell you want to split.

2. Choose Table➪Split Cells or click the Split Cells button on the Tables and Borders toolbars.

3. In the Split Cells dialog box, declare how many cells you want to split the cell into and click OK.

Still in the same vein, you can split a table as well:

1. Place the cursor in what you want to be the first row of the new table.

2. Choose Table➪Split Table.

Using math formulas in tables

No, you don't have to add the figures in columns and rows yourself; Word 97 gladly does that for you. Word 97 can perform other mathematical calculations as well.

To total the figures in a column or row, place the cursor in the cell that is to hold the total and click the AutoSum button on the Tables and Borders toolbar.

The AutoSum button, however, is only good for adding figures. To perform other mathematical calculations and tell Word how to format sums and products:

1. Put the cursor in the cell that will hold the sum or product of the cells above, below, to the right, or to the left.

2. Choose Table➪Formula. The Formula dialog box appears:

Units Sold	Price Unit ($)	Total Sale ($)
13	178.12	
15	179.33	
93	178.00	
31	671.13	
24	411.12	
9	69.13	
11	79.40	
196	1766.23	

Formula

Formula:
`=PRODUCT(left)`

Number format:
`$#,##0.00;($#,##0.00)`

Paste function: Paste bookmark:

OK   Cancel

3. In its wisdom, Word 97 makes a very educated guess about what you want the formula to do and places a formula in the Formula box. If this isn't the formula you want, delete everything except the equal sign in the Formula box, click the down arrow in the Paste Function box, and choose another formula. You may have to type **left, right, above,** or **below** in the parentheses beside the formula to tell Word where the figures that you want it to compute are.

4. In the Number Format box, click the down arrow and choose a format for your number.

5. Click OK.

Word 97 does not calculate blank cells in formulas. Enter a **0** in blank cells if you want them to be included in calculations.

You can copy functions from one cell to another to save yourself the trouble of opening the Formula dialog box.

Decorating a Page with Borders and Backgrounds

Word 97 offers two tools for decorating title pages, certificates, menus, and similar documents: the Format⇨Background command and page borders. One paints a single color or pattern over all the white space on all the pages of a document. The other places borders around the edges of the page. Besides lines, you can decorate the sides of a page with stars, pieces of cake, and other artwork.

The Format⇨Background command goes to work on the entire document. Unfortunately, you can't tell Word to paint a background on a single page or section of a document, so the command is good only for leaflets, fliers, and other one-page documents.

Backgrounds for embellishing pages

To put a color or pattern background on all the pages of a document, choose Format⇨Background and click a background color. Or, to get a pattern, click Fill Effects at the bottom of the menu. You see the Fill Effects dialog box, whose four tabs offer more pattern choices than are available at a wallpaper manufacturers' convention. However you experiment with these patterns, keep your eye on the Sample box in the lower-right corner of the tab. It shows precisely how skillful a decorator you are.

After you select a color or pattern, Word switches to Online Layout view. You can't see backgrounds in any other view. To remove a background, choose Format⇨Background and click the No Fill option.

For this figure, I chose the Diagonal Down Shading style on the Gradient tab of the Fill Effects dialog box.

Putting borders around a page

Here's how to put borders around a page:

1. Click on the page you want to decorate and choose Format⇨Borders and Shading.

2. Click the Page Border tab.

Watch this box!

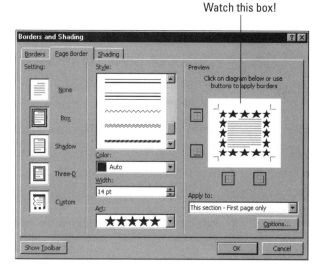

3. Under Setting, choose which kind of border you want. The Custom setting is for putting borders on one, two, or three sides of the page, not four. Use the None setting to remove borders.

4. Under Style, scroll down the list and choose a line for the borders. You will find interesting choices at the bottom of the menu. Be sure to look in the Preview window to see what your choices in this dialog box add up to.

5. Click the Color drop-down menu and choose a color for the borderlines, if you want a color border and you have a color printer.

6. If you chose artwork for the borders, use the Width drop-down menu to tell Word how wide the lines or artwork should be.

7. Click the Art drop-down list and choose a symbol or illustration, if that is what you want for the borders. You will find some amusing choices on this long list, including ice cream cones, bats, and umbrellas.

8. Use the four buttons in the Preview window to tell Word on which sides of the page you want borders. Click these buttons to remove or add borders, as you wish.

9. Under Apply To, tell Word which page or pages in the document get borders.

10. Click the Options button and fill in the Border and Shading Options dialog box if you want to get specific about how close the borders can come to the edge of the page or pages.

11. Click OK.

Drawing in Word 97

Drawing pictures in Word 97 is not for everyone; it's not easy, and getting comfortable with the drawing tools takes a long while. The Drawing toolbar is really a computer program unto itself and is far too complex for this little book. Even if you are not adept with the Drawing toolbar, however, you can use it to decorate newsletters, invitations, and notices with shapes, lines, arrows, and images.

To use the Drawing toolbar, click the Drawing button on the Standard toolbar or right-click a toolbar and choose Drawing from the shortcut menu. Then click on a tool, arrow, or shape to put it on-screen. With the choices on the AutoShapes menu, you can grace the pages of a document with many interesting shapes and images.

To choose a tool or image on the toolbar, click it. The mouse changes into a small cross. Drag the mouse to draw a line or create a shape. By tugging and pulling at the selection handles (the squares at the corners and sides of a shape or line), you can change its shape and size.

To move a shape or line, click it. When the pointer changes into a four-headed arrow, drag the line or image to a new location.

TIP

Personally, I am very fond of the Callouts options on the AutoShapes menu of the Drawing toolbar because I can make use of them along with Word's clip art files to fool people into thinking I am a real cartoonist.

See also "Moving and Resizing Graphics, Text Boxes, and Shapes," also in this part, to learn more about moving and changing the size of shapes and lines on-screen.

Fixing Spacing Problems in Headings

Sometimes when you enlarge text for a heading, one or two letters in the words end up being too close together or too far apart. For example, in the following heading, the *r* and the *n* in *Born* are too close together and almost look like an *m,* and the *T* and *w* in *Twins* are too far apart:

> Twins Born to Mrs. Lin

Adjusting the space between two letters is called *kerning,* and it is easy to do in Word 97:

1. Select the two letters that are too far apart or too close together.

2. Choose Format⇨Font.

3. Click the Character Spacing tab.

4. In the Spacing menu, choose Expanded to spread the letters out or Condensed to pack them in.

5. Word 97 changes the number in the By box for you, but you can do yet more packing or spreading by clicking the down or up arrow yourself.

6. Click the <u>K</u>erning for Fonts check box and enter a point size in the <u>P</u>oints and Above box if you want Word 97 to kern fonts above a certain point size automatically.

7. Click OK.

Including Charts and Graphs in Documents

What is a report without one or two elaborate charts or graphs? It's sort of like an emperor without any clothes on. To put a chart in a report, you can use Word 97's Chart tool. The Chart tool offers 18 kinds of charts, including bar graphs, pie charts, and spider charts.

TIP When you choose the <u>I</u>nsert⇨<u>P</u>icture⇨<u>Ch</u>art command, Word gives you a cumbersome datasheet in which to enter the labels and figures. Rather than enter labels and figures there, however, it is much easier to create a table or use one you've already created, select it, and then choose <u>I</u>nsert⇨<u>P</u>icture⇨<u>Ch</u>art. As the following figure shows, the header rows along the top of the table become the category axis of the chart, the labels in the left-hand column become the chart legend, and the label in the upper-left corner becomes the chart title. For the numbers on the value axis, Word uses the range of numbers on the table.

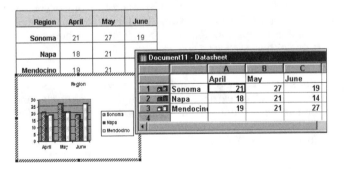

After you've created the chart, delete the table from whence it originated. Then do the following to touch up your chart and make it sing:

✦ **Moving:** To move the chart, click on it. When the cursor changes to a four-headed arrow, drag the chart to a new location.

✦ **Resizing:** To change the chart's size and shape, click on the chart and drag a selection handle (a hollow square on the corner or side). Drag a handle in the corner to change the chart's size but keep its proportions the same; drag a handle on the side to widen or lengthen it. You can do the same to different parts of the chart — the legend, the title — by clicking them and dragging their selection handles.

✦ **Editing:** To change a number or label in a chart, double-click on the chart and then click the View Datasheet button on the Standard toolbar. On the datasheet, erase or enter numbers and labels.

✦ **Changing chart types:** To change the type of chart on display, click the down arrow beside the Chart Type button and choose a new chart type.

✦ **Changing colors:** To change the color of part of a chart, click on it, click the down arrow beside the Fill Color button, and choose a new color. You can also get patterns and textures by clicking the Fill Effects button at the bottom of the drop-down menu.

✦ **Changing fonts:** To change the font of text, double-click it. The Format dialog box appears. Click the Font tab, choose a new font, and click OK.

Inserting Pictures and Graphics in Documents

If you have clip art on your computer, or if you installed the Microsoft clip art library when you installed Microsoft Office, you have a golden opportunity to embellish your documents with art created by genuine artists. You don't have to tell anyone where this art came from, either, as long as you are a good liar.

This entry explains how to insert a clip art image, change its resolutions, and crop it. *See* "Moving and Resizing Graphics, Text Boxes, and Shapes" to learn how to move and change the size and shape of a clip art image after you have inserted it in a document. *See* "Borders and Color Shades for Graphics and Text Boxes" to learn how to do just that. *See* "Wrapping Text around a Text Box or Graphic" to tell Word what nearby text should do when it encounters a graphic on the page.

Inserting a clip art image

To insert a clip art image:

1. Choose Insert➪Picture➪Clip Art. The Microsoft Clip Gallery dialog box appears.

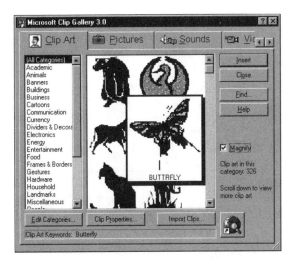

2. Find the clip art file you want to insert. To do that, either click (All Categories) on the Clip Art tab and start scrolling down the images window, or click a category and start scrolling. If you're connected to the Microsoft Network, you can click the globe button in the lower-right corner of the dialog box to scavenge clip art from the Microsoft Web site.

3. When you've found the image you want, click it. To get a better look at an image, you can click the Magnify check box.

4. Click the Insert button to insert the file in your document.

You can also insert a clip art image by choosing Insert⇨Picture⇨ From File and, in the Insert Picture dialog box, finding and double-clicking on the name of the clip art file whose image you want to insert.

Experimenting with brightness and contrast

After you have inserted an image, you can alter it a bit by experimenting with its brightness and contrast. Here's how:

1. Click on the image to select it. You know an image is selected when its square selection handles appear.

2. Choose Format⇨Picture.

3. Under Image control on the Picture tab of the Format object dialog box, change the Brightness and Contrast settings. To do that, either enter percentages in the boxes or move the sliders.

4. Click OK.

For the image on the left, I chose 33 % brightness, 66% contrast; for the one in the middle, 50% brightness, 50% contrast; and for the one on the right, 66% brightness, 33% contrast.

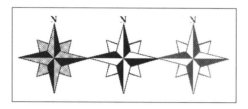

 The other way to change a graphic's brightness and contrast is to select it and click the More Contrast, Less Contrast, More Brightness, or Less Brightness buttons on the Picture toolbar.

Cropping off part of a graphic

You can *crop* — that is, cut off parts of — a graphic, but not very elegantly. To do that, select the graphic and click the Crop button on the Picture toolbar. The pointer changes into an odd shape with two intersecting triangles on it. Move the pointer to a selection handle and start dragging. The dotted line tells you what part of the graphic you are cutting off. Sorry, you can only crop off sides of the graphic. You can't cut a circle out of the middle, for example, proving once again that the computer will never replace that ancient and noble device, the scissors.

Keeping Paragraphs and Lines Together

Where pages break in a document matters a lot. If a figure is on one page and its caption is on the next, or a heading falls at the very bottom of a page and doesn't have any text underneath it, or a chapter title appears at the bottom of a page, the readers of your document will be sorely inconvenienced. You can prevent these problems, however, with the four check boxes in the Pagination area of the Line and Page Breaks tab of the Paragraph dialog box.

Paragraph	? X
Indents and Spacing **Line and Page Breaks**	
Pagination	
☑ Widow/Orphan control ☐ Keep with next	
☐ Keep lines together ☐ Page break before	

To make sure that a chapter title or heading appears at the top of a page:

1. Click in the chapter title or heading.

2. Choose Format⇨Paragraph.

3. Click the Line and Page Breaks tab.

4. Choose Page Break before.

5. Click OK.

To make sure that text lines, a heading, and the following paragraph, paragraphs, or graphics stay on the same page:

1. Select the text lines. If you want to keep paragraphs together, either place the cursor in the paragraph that you want to tie to the following paragraph, or select all the paragraphs except the last one.

2. Choose Format⇨Paragraph.

3. Click the Line and Page Breaks tab.

4. Click a Pagination check box:

- **Keep Lines Together:** Prevents the lines you selected from being broken across two pages.

- **Keep with Next:** Ties the paragraph or paragraphs to the paragraph that follows so that they all stay on the same page.

5. Click OK.

Word 97 sometimes has to break a page early to make all your paragraphs and text stay together on the next page. That can create a lot of empty, forlorn white space.

What's more, forgetting where and when you choose Pagination options in a document is easy. If you notice pages breaking in weird places, click the Show/Hide ¶ button and look for small black squares in the margin. These squares represent pagination codes. You can always "deselect" Pagination options by opening the Paragraph dialog box and removing the check marks from the Pagination check boxes.

Whatever you do, don't remove the check mark from the Widow/Orphan control check box in the Line and Page Breaks tab. This option keeps widows and orphans from appearing in documents. A *widow* is a very short line, usually one word, that appears at the end of a paragraph. Widows create a lot of ugly white space across the page. An *orphan* is a single line of text at the start of a paragraph that appears at the very bottom of a page. Orphans sort of cheat the reader, because the reader can't tell how long the paragraph is until he or she turns the page.

"Landscape" Documents

A *landscape* document is one in which the page is wider than it is long, like a painting of a landscape. Most documents, like the pages of this book, are printed in portrait style, with the short sides of the page on the top and bottom. However, creating a landscape document is a good idea because a landscape document stands out from the usual crowd of portrait documents.

To turn the page on its ear and create a landscape document, follow these steps:

1. Choose File⇨Page Setup.

2. Click the Paper Size tab.

3. In the Orientation area, click the Landscape option button. The piece of paper in the Preview box turns on its side.

4. In the Apply to box, choose Whole Document to print landscape pages throughout the document, This Section to print only the section the cursor is in, or This Point Forward to make the rest of the pages in the document landscape pages.

5. Click OK.

See also "Printing on Different-Sized Paper," in Part IV, to learn other ways of creating documents on different paper sizes and shapes.

Moving and Resizing Graphics, Text Boxes, and Shapes

After you've put an object — a graphic, text box, or AutoShape — in a document, it's time to start manipulating it. This entry explains how to slide an object up or down or side to side on a page. It also explains how to twist and bend objects into different shapes.

See also "Wrapping Text Around Graphics and Text" at the end of this part to learn how to tell Word 97 what nearby text should do when it bumps against an object.

Moving an object on the page

Moving an object on a page is easy enough. All you have to do is click on the graphic, text box, shape, or AutoShape. Very shortly, if you are not moving a text box, selection handles appear and the pointer changes into a four-headed arrow. If you are moving a text box, place the pointer on the perimeter of the box to see the four-headed arrow.

Next, drag the pointer where you want the object to be on the page. Dotted lines show where you are moving it. When it's in the right position, release the mouse button.

Changing an object's size and shape

How you change an object's size depends on whether you want to keep its proportions:

✦ **Changing size but not proportions:** To change the size of an object but keep its proportions, click on the object and move the cursor to one of the selection handles on the *corners*. The cursor changes into a double-headed arrow. Click and start dragging. Dotted lines show how you are changing the size of the frame. When it's the right size, release the mouse button.

✦ **Changing size and proportions:** To change both the size of an object *and* its proportions, move the cursor to a selection handle on the *side*. When the cursor changes into a double-headed arrow, click and start dragging. Dotted lines show how the object is being changed. When it is the size and shape you want, release the mouse button.

This illustration shows the same graphic at three different sizes. The original graphic is on the left. For the middle graphic, I pulled a corner selection handle to enlarge it but keep its proportions. For the one on the right, I pulled a selection handle on the side to enlarge it and change its proportions.

TIP

If you want to get very specific about how big a graphic or text box is, go to the Size tab of the Format dialog box. To do that, choose Format⇨Picture or Format⇨Text Box and click the Size tab. Then enter measurements in the Height and Width boxes. Go this route if you want to make text boxes or graphics the same size.

"Watermarking" for the Elegant Effect

A *watermark* is a pale image that appears behind text. True watermarks are made in the paper mold and can be seen only when the sheet of paper is held up to a light. You can't make true watermarks with Word 97, but you can make the closest thing to them that can be attained in the debased digital world in which we live.

To make a watermark like the one shown here, start by inserting the graphic image that is to form the watermark. (*See also* "Inserting Pictures and Graphics in Documents" earlier in this part to find out how to do that. *See also* "Anchoring Text and Graphics" at the start of this part to make the watermark stay in one place on the page, perhaps in the middle or corner.)

After you have created and formatted the graphic, follow these steps to create a watermark:

1. Click on the graphic image to select it.

2. Choose Format⇨Picture.

3. Under Image control on the Picture tab of the Format Picture dialog box, click the Color drop-down menu and choose Watermark.

4. Click the Wrapping tab and, under Wrapping style, click the None box.

5. Click OK to close the Format Picture dialog box. Back on-screen, the graphic is still selected and you can still see its square selection handles.

6. Right-click on the graphic and choose Order⇨Send Behind Text from the shortcut menu.

There you have it, a digital watermark. When you type text, it appears on top of the watermark.

WordArt for Embellishing Documents

You can bend, spindle, and mutilate text with a feature called WordArt. I believe this feature was inspired by old superhero comics, in which words and images that may have come from the WordArt Gallery appeared whenever Batman, Spiderman, and Wonder Woman brawled with the criminal element.

WordArt, a memory hog, makes computers run very slowly. Don't experiment with WordArt if you are in a hurry or your computer lacks memory.

To create a WordArt image, put the cursor roughly where you want it to go and do the following:

1. Choose Insert⇨Picture⇨WordArt. You see the WordArt Gallery.

![WordArt Gallery dialog box showing a grid of WordArt styles. Select a WordArt style: five columns by five rows of sample text styles, with OK and Cancel buttons.]

2. Click the image that strikes your fancy and then click OK.

3. In the Edit WordArt Text dialog box, type a word or words of your own and click OK.

The image arrives on-screen with its selection handles showing. WordArt images can be moved and manipulated just like graphic images. To really bend the word or words out of shape, click and drag the yellow diamond on the image. To change the wording, click Edit Te_x_t on the WordArt toolbar to reopen the Edit WordArt Text dialog box.

Working with Text Boxes

Put text in a text box when you want it to stand out on the page. Text boxes can be shaded, filled with color, and given borders. What's more, you can move one around at will on the page until it lands in the right place. You can even make text jump from one text box to the next in a document — a nice feature, for example, when you want a newsletter article on page 1 to be continued on page 2. Instead of cutting and pasting text from page 1 to page 2, Word 97 moves the text for you as the column on page 1 fills up.

See also these entries in this part that pertain to text boxes: "Borders and Color Shades for Graphics and Text Boxes," "Moving and Resizing Graphics, Text Boxes, and Shapes," and "Wrapping Text around a Text Box or Graphic."

Inserting a text box

To put a text box in a document, follow these steps:

1. Choose _I_nsert⇨Te_x_t Box or click the Text Box button on the Drawing toolbar. The pointer turns into a cross.

2. Click and drag to draw the text box. Lines show you how big it will be when you release the mouse button.

3. Release the mouse button.

After you've inserted the text box, you can type text in it and call on all the formatting techniques in Word 97 to boldface it, align it, or do what you will with it.

Changing the direction of the text

On the Text Box toolbar is a little toy called the Change Text Direction button. Click a text box and click this button to make the text in the text box change orientation. Here, you can see what happens when you click the Change Text Direction button.

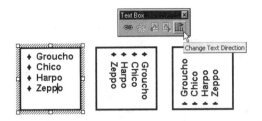

Linking the text in different text boxes

As I mentioned earlier, you can link text boxes so that the text in the first box is pushed into the next one when it fills up. To link text boxes, start by creating all the text boxes you will need. You cannot link text boxes that already have text in them. Use these buttons on the Text Box toolbar to link the text boxes in a document:

✦ **Create Text Box Link:** Click a text box and then click this button to create a forward link. When you click the button, the pointer changes into a very odd-looking pointer that looks something like a Spanish galleon. Move the odd-looking pointer to the next text box in the chain and click there to create a link.

✦ **Break Forward Link:** To break a link, click the text box that is to be the last in the chain, and then click the Break Forward Link button.

✦ **Previous Text Box and Next Text Box:** Click these buttons to go backwards or forwards through the text boxes in the chain.

Wrapping Text around a Text Box or Graphic

Word 97 gives you lots of interesting opportunities to wrap text around the text boxes and graphics in a document. By playing with the different ways to wrap text, you can create very sophisticated layouts.

When you wrap text, you pick a wrapping style and the side of the text box or graphic around which to wrap the text. The Wrapping style choices are Square, Tight, Through, None, and Top & Bottom. The Wrap to choices are Both Sides, Left, Right, and Largest Side. On the theory that a picture is worth a thousand words, the following figure demonstrates 9 of the 14 possible Wrapping Style and Wrap To combinations.

The None and Through wrapping styles, and the Largest Side Wrap to option, are confusing. None does not wrap the text at all — the text gets hidden behind the text box or graphic. Through is for wrapping text around odd-shaped graphics. It allows text to get closer to the graphic than is usually allowed. As the figure shows, the Largest Side Wrap to option wraps the text around the side of the graphic that allows the most room for wrapping, and it leaves empty space to the narrow side of the graphic.

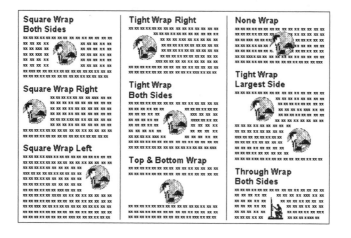

Wrapped text looks best when it is justified and hyphenated. That way, text can get closer to the text box or graphic that is being "wrapped."

To wrap text around a graphic or text box:

1. Select the text box or graphic by clicking it.

2. Choose Format⟿Text Box or Format⟿Picture (if you're dealing with a graphic).

3. Click the Wrapping tab in the Format dialog box.

4. Click a box under Wrapping Style to tell Word how you want the text to behave when it reaches the graphic or text box.

5. Under Wrap To, tell Word which side or sides of the text box or graphic to wrap the text around.

6. Under Distance from Text, change the settings if you want to get specific about how close text can come to the graphic or text box.

7. Click OK.

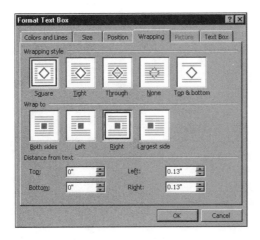

Fancy and Esoteric Stuff

Everything in Part VII deserves a "Cool Stuff" icon. You find instructions here for doing tasks that would take hours and hours without Word 97's help. Most of the tasks have to do with generating lists of one kind or another — tables of contents, tables of figures, and indexes. You also find some neat shortcuts for tracking changes to documents and writing commentary on documents.

In this part . . .

- ✔ Commenting on a document
- ✔ Generating tables of contents, tables of figures, and other tables
- ✔ Creating an index
- ✔ Tracking revisions made to documents
- ✔ Creating and working with footnotes, endnotes, and cross-references
- ✔ Creating a Web page

Commenting on a Document

In the old days, comments were scribbled illegibly in the margins of books and documents, but in Word 97, comments are easy to read. Where comments have been made in a document, the text is highlighted. As shown here, all you have to do is move the cursor over the highlighted text to read the comment and the name of the person who made it:

> **Anne Crowley:**
> Re this whole paragraph: Has
> he gone mental?
>
> Furthermore, the unemployment rate among spies has skyrocketed since the end of the Cold War. Perfectly talented individuals — women and men capable of wire-tapping a building in, say, a matter of minutes — have nowhere to sell their services. Surely we can

If you are putting together a proposal, you can pass it around the office and invite everyone to comment on it. If someone makes an especially good comment, you can include it in the main text merely by copying and pasting it.

To write a comment:

1. Select the word or sentence that you want to criticize or praise.

2. Choose <u>I</u>nsert⇨Co<u>mm</u>ent. A window opens at the bottom of the screen with comments that have already been made and the initials of the people who made them. The comments are numbered.

Click to see comments by individual reviewers

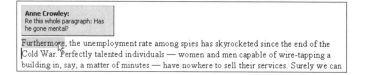

> Furthermore [AC1], the unemployment rate among spies has skyrocketed since the end of the Cold War. Perfectly talented individuals — women and men capable of wire-tapping a building in, say, a matter of minutes — have nowhere to sell their services. Surely we can seek out and recruit these individuals for our own efforts. After all, industrial espionage is the only game in town, now that intragovernment [PW2] espionage has [AC3] bit the dust [AC4].
>
> Comments From: [All Reviewers] [Close]
>
> [AC1]Re this whole paragraph: Has he gone mental?
> [PW2] Intragovernment espionage? What's that, like Spy vs. Spy?
> [AC3]
> [AC4]Now he's talking sense!

3. Type your comment next to the square brackets with your initials in them. (If your initials don't appear in the brackets, choose <u>T</u>ools⇨<u>O</u>ptions, click the User Information tab, and type your initials in the <u>I</u>nitials box.)

4. Click the <u>C</u>lose button.

TIP

Besides placing the cursor on a highlighted comment to read it, you can read the entire list of comments by choosing View⊃Comments. Click on a comment in the Comment window, and the document window scrolls to the place in the text where the comment was made.

If a comment is so good that it belongs in the document, simply select it in the Comment window, drag it into the document, and reformat or rewrite it as necessary.

To delete a comment, right-click its highlighting in the text and choose Delete Comment from the shortcut menu. The remaining annotations are renumbered. Unfortunately, you can't delete all the comments in a document at the same time, so you should delete them one at a time as you finish reviewing them. Choose Edit Comment from the shortcut menu to open the Comments window and alter a comment.

Creating a Table of Figures, Graphs, and More

A table of figures, graphs, equations, illustrations, listings, programs, or tables sometimes appears at the start of technical documents and scholarly papers so that readers can quickly refer to figures, graphs, or whatnot. In Word 97, you can create tables of all the items in the aforementioned list. To do so, however, you must have used the Insert⊃Caption command to create the captions for the figures, graphs, and so on. (*See* "Putting Captions on Figures and Tables" later in Part VII if you'd like Word 97's help with captions.)

To generate the table:

1. Put the cursor where you want the table to go.

2. Choose Insert⊃Index and Tables.

3. Click the Table of Figures tab.

Index and Tables   **? ☒**

| Index | Table of Contents | Table of Figures | Table of Authorities |

Caption label:

Illustration
Listing
Program

Preview

Listing 1: Text *1*
Listing 2: Text *3*
Listing 3: Text *5*
Listing 4: Text *7*
Listing 5: Text *10*

OK

Cancel

Formats:

From template
Classic
Distinctive
Centered

Options...

Modify...

☑ Show page numbers   ☑ Include label and number

☑ Right align page numbers   Tab leader: .... ▼

4. Choose options on the tab. As you do so, watch the Preview box to see how your choices affect the table's appearance:

- **Caption Label:** Choose what kind of table you're creating.

- **Formats:** Choose a format from the list if you don't want to use the one from the template.

- **Show Page Numbers:** Includes page numbers in the table.

- **Right Align Page Numbers:** Aligns the numbers along the right side of the table so that the ones and tens line up under each other.

- **Include Label and Number:** Includes the word *Equation, Figure, Graph, Illustration, Listing, Program,* or *Table,* as well as the number or letter in the table caption.

- **Tab Leader:** Choose another leader, or no leader at all, if you don't want a line of periods to appear between the caption and the number of the page on which it appears.

- **Options:** Lets you create tables from the styles used in your document or the fields found in the tables.

- **Modify:** You can modify the template's table format by clicking the Modify button and creating a new table style of your own. *See* "Using styles for consistent formatting" in Part III to see how to create a new style.

5. Click OK when you're done.

If you add a figure, graph, or whatnot to the document, or if you remove one, you can easily get an up-to-date table. Click in the table and press F9, or right-click in the table and choose Update Field from the shortcut menu. A dialog box asks how to update the table. Choose one of these options and click OK:

- ✦ **Update Page Numbers Only:** Choose this option to put up-to-date page numbers in the table. New figures, graphics, and whatnot that you added do not appear in the table, nor do figures, graphics and so on that you deleted get dropped from it. This option is strictly for handling page numbers.

- ✦ **Update Entire Table:** Choose this option to get a revamped, entirely up-to-date table. New figures, graphics, or whatnot are added to the table, and figures, graphics, or whatnot that you deleted are removed.

Creating Your Own Web Page

In the future, everyone will be famous for fifteen minutes, and everyone will have a Web page. Looking toward the future, Word 97 offers commands for creating a Web page from scratch and for converting a Word document into an HTML document that Web browsers can read.

Web browsers are the computer applications that connect to Web sites and display Web pages. A Web browser cannot "see" images and text or display them on a computer screen unless the images and text have been tagged with *hypertext markup language* (HTML) codes. Fortunately for you and for the teeming multitudes who will admire your Web pages, Word 97 has made the dreary task of entering HTML codes very easy: Word 97 can do it for you. It can code a document and do a good job of it, as long as you thoughtfully assign styles to the different parts of the document. When Word converts a document to HTML, it converts styles to HTML codes.

Not all Word styles can be converted to HTML codes. Captions, footnotes, borders, and shading, for example, are not on speaking terms with HTML. And to convert Word documents to Web pages, the Microsoft Internet Explorer must have been installed on your computer.

See "Hyperlinking in Word 97," also in this part, to learn how to create hyperlinks for your Web pages. *See also* "Using styles for consistent formatting" in Part III to learn about styles.

Creating a Web page from scratch

To create a Web page from scratch, use the Web Page Wizard:

1. Choose File⇨New.

2. Click the Web Pages tab in the New dialog box.

3. Double-click the Web Page Wizard icon. After a moment, you see a prototype Web page and the Web Page Wizard dialog box.

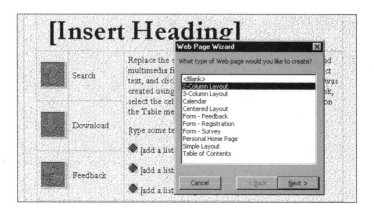

4. Click the type of Web page you would like to create. The prototype in the background changes so you can see what your Web page choice looks like. Click another type of Web page if you want.

5. Click Next. The Web Page Wizard asks what visual style to use for the Web page.

6. Choose a visual style. Again, the prototype changes so you can see precisely what the style you chose is. Click another visual style if you wish.

7. Click the Finish button.

8. Follow the directions on the Web page itself to enter the text, graphics, and hyperlinks.

Converting Word documents to Web pages

To convert a Word document to a Web page:

1. Open the document to be converted to an HTML document.

2. Choose File➪Save as HTML.

3. In the Save As HTML dialog box, find the folder that will hold your HTML file, enter a name in the File Name box, and click Save. Word gives the file the *.html* extension. When next you see the file, it appears in Online Layout View.

4. Click the Web Page Preview button or choose File➪Web Page Preview to see what your new HTML document looks like to someone viewing it by means of a Web browser. Microsoft's Web browser, the Microsoft Internet Explorer, opens and you see your Web page in all its glory.

5. To get back to Word 97 and make changes to the original HTML document, click the Edit button or choose <u>E</u>dit⇨Cu<u>r</u>rent Page and make your changes.

Hereafter when you make changes to the original document, click the Save button before you click the Web Page Preview button to find out what your editorial changes do to the Web page. By going back and forth between the Web page and its Word 97 original, you can create a very handsome Web page.

Generating a Table of Contents

 A book-size document isn't worth very much without a table of contents. How else can readers find what they're looking for? Generating a table of contents with Word 97 is easy, as long as you give the headings in the document different styles — Heading 1, Heading 2, and so on.

 Before you create your TOC, create a new section in which to put it and number the pages in the new section with Roman numerals. TOCs, including the TOC in this book, are usually numbered in this way. The first entry in the TOC should cite page number 1. If you don't take my advice and create a new section, the TOC will occupy the first few numbered pages of your document, and the number scheme will be thrown off.

To create a table of contents:

1. Place the cursor where you want the TOC to go.

2. Choose <u>I</u>nsert⇨In<u>d</u>ex and Tables.

3. Click the Table of <u>C</u>ontents tab in the Index and Tables dialog box.

Index and Tables	? ✕
<u>I</u>ndex │ Table of <u>C</u>ontents │ Table of <u>F</u>igures │ Table of <u>A</u>uthorities	
For<u>m</u>ats:	Pre<u>v</u>iew
From template	
Classic	HEADING 1 -------------------1
Distinctive	
Fancy	
Modern	**Heading 2** -----------------------3
Formal	Heading 3------------------------5
Simple	
✓ <u>S</u>how page numbers	Show <u>l</u>evels: 3
✓ <u>R</u>ight align page numbers	Ta<u>b</u> leader: ------- ▼
	OK │ Cancel │ <u>O</u>ptions... │ <u>M</u>odify...

4. Choose options in the dialog box. As you do so, watch the Preview box as you do so to see what effect your choices have.

5. Click OK when you're done.

The Table of Contents tab gives you lots of ways to control what goes in your TOC and what it looks like:

✦ **Show Page Numbers:** Uncheck this box if you want your TOC to be a simple list that doesn't refer to headings by page.

✦ **Right Align Page Numbers:** Aligns the page numbers along the right side of the TOC so that the ones and tens line up under one another.

✦ **Show Levels:** Determines how many heading levels are included in the TOC. Unless your document is a legal contract or other formal paper, enter a **2** or **3** here. A TOC is supposed to help readers find information quickly. Including lots of headings that take a long time to read through defeats the purpose of having a TOC.

✦ **Tab Leader:** A *leader* is the punctuation mark that appears between the heading and the page number the heading is on. If you don't want periods as the leader, choose another leader or choose (none).

✦ **Options:** Opens the Table of Contents Options dialog box so you can create TOC entries from the styles in your document. Click this button if you've created a Chapter Title style, for example. Scroll down the TOC Level box to find the style you want to include and type a level number in the box beside its name. Chapter titles should be given the 1 level. You can also include text in fields in the TOC by clicking the Table Entry Fields check box. Index entries and tables of figures, for example, can be included in the TOC with this check box. Click Reset if you get all tangled up and want to start over.

✦ **Modify:** Click this button if none of the TOC formats in the Formats box suits you and you want to try your hand at inventing a TOC style of your own. If you're adventurous enough to get this far, you probably already know how to create a new style. If you don't, *see* "Using styles for consistent formatting" in Part III.

Hidden Text and Secret Messages

Besides writing comments to critique a document, you can critique a document with hidden text. (Comments are explained at the start of this part.) Hidden text is not printed along with other text unless you tell Word 97 to print it. All you have to do to see hidden text is click the Show/Hide ¶ button.

To write hidden text and secret messages in a document:

1. Place the cursor where you want the text to go.

2. Choose Format⇨Font.

3. In the Effects area in the middle of the Font dialog box, click the Hidden check box.

4. Click the OK button.

5. Type your secret message.

Dotted lines appear below hidden text on-screen. This advertising copywriter used hidden text to show the subliminal messages that the advertisement is meant to convey:

> Summer's coming on and that means bathing suit time again and you put on weight since last summer, no doubt. Why not come visit us at the Hayes Street Workout Center? You'll meet lots of friendly people i.e., attractive members of the opposite sex. Come on. You've got nothing to lose — nothing but a few pounds, that is.¶

To see hidden text, either click the Show/Hide ¶ button or choose Tools⇨Options, click the View tab, and click the Hidden Text check box in the Nonprinting characters area of the dialog box. When it's time to hide the text again, either click the Show/Hide ¶ button or open the Options dialog box and remove the check mark from the Hidden Text check box on the View tab.

Hyperlinking in Word 97

A *hyperlink* is a shortcut from one place to another in the same document or from one document to another document entirely. If you've fooled around in Word's Help program or explored the Internet, you have already discovered hyperlinks. When you click a hyperlink, it takes you elsewhere — to another help file if you are inside the Help program, or to another Web page if you surfing the Internet. You can always tell when the pointer has moved over a hyperlink because it changes into a gloved hand with a pointing finger. Hyperlinks are blue on-screen. In Word 97, you also see a yellow box that lists the file path that the hyperlink travels to get you from one place to another:

> C:\ZOldStuff\Computer\Word 97QR\IDG files\~$Hyper2.doc
>
> Our marketing group tested an assortment of Dummies®.

In Word 97, you can link to Internet addresses (also known as *uniform resource locators,* or URLs), documents on your computer, and documents on a network to which your computer is connected. Before you create a hyperlink to a URL, make sure you know its address or have visited it before. After you click a hyperlink and go to a new place, the Web toolbar appears on-screen. By clicking buttons on the Web toolbar, you can go back and forth among the hyperlinks you've visited or travel instantly to new hyperlink destinations.

Creating a hyperlink

To create a hyperlink to another place in the same document or to a specific place in another document, insert a bookmark (with the Insert⇨Bookmark command) where you want the hyperlink to take you. Without bookmarks, a hyperlink goes directly to the top of the document to which the link has been made. Follow these steps to create a hyperlink:

1. Save the file.

2. Select the word or phrase in your document that is to signal the hyperlink. When you are done creating the link, the word or phrase will appear in blue, and the cursor will change to a pointing hand when you slide the pointer over the word or phrase.

3. Choose Insert⇨Hyperlink or press Ctrl+K. You see the Insert Hyperlink dialog box.

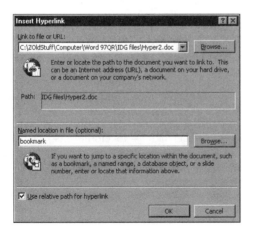

4. If you are establishing a link to another place in the same document, you needn't enter anything in the Link to File or URL list box. Otherwise, do the following:

- **Another document:** To make a link to another document, click the Browse button beside the Link to File or URL list box. You see the Link to File dialog box. Treat this dialog box as you would the Open dialog box and find the file to which you want to establish the link. When have found and selected the file, click OK.

- **URL address:** To link to a URL address, either type an address in the Link to File or URL list box (type **http://www.idgbooks.com**, for example), or else select a URL from the drop-down list.

5. To make a link to a new place in the document you are working in or to a specific place in another document, click the Browse button beside the Named Location in File list box. You see the Bookmark dialog box. Click on the bookmark the hyperlink is to go to and click OK.

6. Make sure the check mark remains in the Use Relative Path For Hyperlink check box. By keeping the check mark there, you can re-establish the hyperlink if you move the target file later on.

7. Click OK.

Suppose you move the file to which you've established the hyperlink. To make the hyperlink work again, right-click it and choose Hyperlink⇨Edit Hyperlink from the shortcut menu. Then, in the Edit Hyperlink dialog box, establish the link all over again the same way you did when you created the hyperlink in the first place.

To remove a hyperlink, right-click it, choose Hyperlink⇨Edit Hyperlink, and click the Remove Link button in the Edit Hyperlink dialog box.

Traveling from hyperlink to hyperlink

As you know already, you click a blue hyperlink to jump to its target file or destination. After you make the jump, the hyperlink changes colors from blue to magenta to let you know that you've "been there, done that." By clicking the Back and Forward buttons on the Web toolbar, you can go back and forth among the hyperlinks you've traveled to.

The Web toolbar offers other means of traveling from hyperlink to hyperlink. To display the Web toolbar, right-click on a toolbar and choose Web. Click the list box and buttons on the Web toolbar to travel from place to place in hyperlinked documents or visit the World Wide Web:

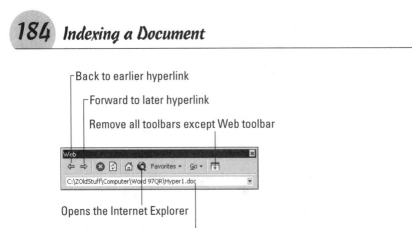

Back to earlier hyperlink

Forward to later hyperlink

Remove all toolbars except Web toolbar

Opens the Internet Explorer

Lists documents and Web sites you can go back to

Indexing a Document

A good index is a thing of beauty. User manuals, reference works of any length, and reports that readers will refer to all require indexes. Except for the table of contents, the only way to find information in a long document is to look in the index.

An index entry can be formatted in many ways. You can cross-reference index entries, list a page range in an index entry, and break out an index entry into subentries and sub-subentries. To help you with your index, this figure explains indexing terminology:

Subentries

Cross-reference

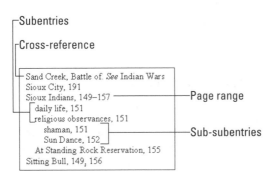

Page range

Sub-subentries

Writing a good index entry is as hard as writing good, descriptive headings. As you enter index entries in your document, ask yourself how you would look up information in the index if you were reading it, and enter your index entries accordingly.

Marking index items in the document

Marking index items yourself is easier than it seems. Once you open the Mark Index Entry dialog box, it stays open so that you can scroll through your document and make entries.

1. If you see a word in your document that you can use as a main, top-level entry, select it. You can save a little time that way, as you see shortly. Otherwise, if you don't see a word you can use, place the cursor in the paragraph or heading whose topic you want to include in the index.

2. Press Alt+Shift+X. The Mark Index Entry dialog box appears. If you selected a word, it appears in the Main Entry box.

Sub-subentry ┐

3. Choose how you want to handle this index entry. When you enter the text, don't put a comma or period after it. Word 97 does that when it generates the index. The text you enter will appear in your index.

- **Main entry:** If you're entering a main, top-level entry, either leave the text in the Main Entry box (if it's already there), type new text to describe this entry, or edit the text that's already there. Leave the Subentry box blank.

- **Subentry:** To create a subentry, enter text in the Subentry box. The text will appear in the index below the Main Entry text, so make sure that there is text in the Main Entry box and that the subentry text fits under the main entry.

- **Sub-subentry:** A sub-subentry is the third level in the hierarchy. To create a sub-subentry, type the subentry, enter a colon (:), and type the sub-subentry.

4. Decide how to handle the page reference in the entry:

- **Cross-reference:** To go without a page reference and refer the reader to another index entry, click <u>C</u>ross-reference and type the other entry in the text box after the word *See.* What you type here appears in your index, so be sure that the topic you refer the reader to is really in the index.

- **Current <u>P</u>age:** Click this option to enter a single page number after the entry.

- **<u>P</u>age Range:** Click this option if you're indexing a subject that covers several pages in your document. A page range index entry looks something like this: "Sioux Indians, 45–49." To make a page range entry, you must create a bookmark for the range. Click outside the dialog box to get back to your document and select all the text in the page range. Then choose <u>I</u>nsert⇨Boo<u>k</u>mark, type a name in the Bookmark name box (you may as well type the name of the index entry) and click <u>A</u>dd. Back in the Mark Entry dialog box, click the Page <u>R</u>ange option button, click the down arrow, and choose your bookmark from the list. Click <u>M</u>ark when you get to Step 6, not Mark <u>A</u>ll.

5. You can boldface or italicize a page number or page range by clicking the Page number format check box. In some indexes, the page or page range where the topic is explained in the most depth is italicized or boldfaced so that readers can get to the juiciest parts first.

6. If you selected a word in Step 1, you can click Mark <u>A</u>ll to have Word 97 go through the document and mark all words identical to the one in the Main <u>E</u>ntry box. Click <u>M</u>ark to put this single entry in the index.

7. Click outside the Mark Index Entry dialog and find the next topic or word you want to mark for the index.

8. Repeat Steps 3 through 7 until you've marked all your index entries, and then click Close to close the Mark Index Entry dialog box.

A bunch of ugly field codes appear in your document. You can render them invisible by clicking the Show/Hide ¶ button. Now you can go ahead and generate the index.

Generating an index

After you mark the index entries, it's time to generate the index:

1. Place the cursor where you want the index to go, most likely at the end of the document. You might type the word **Index** and format the word in a decorative way.

2. Choose Insert⇨Index and Tables and click the Index tab, if necessary.

3. Choose options in Index tab of the Index and Tables dialog box. As you do so, watch the Preview box to see what happens.

Watch this box!

| Index and Tables | ? X |

Index | Table of Contents | Table of Figures | Table of Authorities

Type
○ Indented
○ Run-in

Formats:
Modern
Bulleted
Formal
Simple

☐ Headings for accented letters   Columns: 2

☐ Right align page numbers   Tab leader:

Preview
A
Aristotle, 2
Asteroid belt. *See* Jupiter
Atmosphere
Earth
exosphere, 4
ionosphere, 3

OK
Cancel
Mark Entry...
AutoMark...
Modify...

4. When you're done, click OK.

Here are the options on the Index tab of the Index and Tables dialog box:

✦ **Type:** Choose Run-in if you want subentries and sub-subentries to appear flush with the left margin like main entries. Otherwise, stick with the Indented option to indent them.

✦ **Formats:** Word 97 offers a number of attractive index layouts. You can choose one from the list.

✦ **Headings for Accented Letters:** Places entries that begin with accented letters after entries that begin with unaccented letters. For example, "Ängstrom, Harry, 134" goes before "Atwater, Lee, 112," unless you check this box, in which case "Ängstrom, Harry, 134" and all other *A* entries with accents and other weird marks go after the other *A* entries.

✦ **Right Align Page Numbers:** Normally, page numbers appear right after entries and are separated from entries by a comma, but you can right-align the entries so they line up under one another with this option.

✦ **Columns:** Stick with 2, unless you don't have subentries or sub-subentries and you can squeeze three columns on the page.

✦ **Tab Leader:** Some index formats (such as Formal) place a *leader* between the entry and the page number. A leader is a series of dots or dashes. If you're working with a format that has a leader, you can choose a leader from the drop-down list.

✦ **Modify:** Click this button if you're adventurous and want to create an index style of your own. You must choose From Template in the Formats box in order to do so. In the Style dialog box, choose an Index level style, and then click the Style dialog box's Modify button to get to the Modify Style dialog box and create a style of your own. *See* "Using styles for consistent formatting" in Part III if you need help with creating styles.

To update an index after you create or delete entries, either right-click the index and then choose Update Field from the shortcut menu, or click the index and press F9.

Editing an index

After you generate an index, read it carefully to make sure all entries are useful to readers. Inevitably, something doesn't come out right, but you can edit index entries as you would the text in a document. Index field markers are enclosed in angle brackets with the letters *XE* and the text of the index entry in quotation marks, like so: { XE: "Sioux Indians:sun dance" }. To edit an index marker, click the Show/Hide ¶ button to see the field markers and find the one you need to edit. Then delete letters or type letters as you would normal text.

You can use the Edit⇨Find command to look for index entries. Word finds those as well as text.

Putting Captions on Figures and Tables

Word 97 has a special feature for putting captions on tables, figures, equations, graphs, and a number of other things. Of course, you can add captions yourself, but by letting Word 97 do it, you can compile the captions in tables. At the beginning of a user manual, for example, you can have a table called "Figures in This Manual." Readers can refer to the table when they want to find a figure.

To put a caption on a figure, table, equation, graph, or just about anything else for that matter:

1. Either place the cursor where you want the caption to go or select the item for which you want to write a caption.

2. Choose Insert⇨Caption. The Caption dialog box appears.

3. Write a caption in the Caption box.

4. In the Label drop-down list, choose which kind of item you're creating a caption for. To create a caption for something that is not on the list, click the New Label button, type a label in the Label box, and click OK.

5. If you selected the item before you chose Insert⇨Caption, choose Below Selected Item or Above Selected Item in the Position drop-down list.

6. Click the Numbering button if you want a different numbering scheme than the one shown in the Caption box. In the Caption Numbering dialog box, choose a number scheme from the Format menu and look at the examples at the bottom to see what your choices mean. Click the Include Chapter Number check box and choose a style and separator if you want to include chapter numbers in the numbering scheme. Click OK to get back to the Caption dialog box.

7. Click the AutoCaption button if you want Word 97 to put captions on new tables, equations, or whatever as you create them. The AutoCaption dialog box appears if you make this choice. Click an item in the Add Caption When Inserting box and click OK.

8. Click OK to insert your caption.

See "Creating a Table of Figures, Graphs, and More" earlier in this part to see how to compile the captions in a table.

Putting Cross-References in a Document

Cross-references are very handy indeed. They tell readers where to go to find more information on a topic. The problem with cross-references, however, is that the thing being cross-referenced really has to be there. If you send readers to a heading called "The Cat's Pajamas" on page 93 and neither the heading nor the page exists, readers curse and tell you where to go, instead of the other way around.

Fortunately for you, Word 97 lets you know when you make errant cross-references. You can refer readers to headings, page numbers, footnotes, endnotes, and plain old paragraphs. And as long you create captions for your cross-references with the Insert⇨Caption command, you can also make cross-references to equations, figures, graphs, listings, programs, and tables. If you delete the thing that a cross-reference refers to and render the cross-reference invalid, Word 97 tells you about it the next time you update your cross-references. Best of all, if the page number, numbered item, or text that a cross-reference refers to changes, so does the cross-reference.

You can refer to text in documents other than the one you're working on, as long as both documents are part of the same master document (*see* "Master Document for Really Big Jobs" in Part V to learn about master documents).

To create a cross-reference:

1. Write the first part of the cross-reference text. For example, you could write **To learn more about these cowboys of the pampas, see page** and then enter a blank space. The blank space separates the word *page* from the page number you're about to enter with the Insert⇨Cross-reference command. If you are referring to a heading, write something like **For more information, see "**. Don't enter a blank space this time because the heading text will appear right after the double-quotation mark.

2. Choose Insert⇨Cross-reference. The Cross-reference dialog box appears:

Cross-reference		? ☒
Reference type:	Insert reference to:	
Heading ▼	Heading text ▼	
☑ Insert as hyperlink	☐ Include above/below	
For which heading:		
The Gouchos: A Dying Breed		
Intrigue on the Pampas		
Was Borges Right?		
Roll on Rio Plata		
The Long Night		
War with Uruguay		
How the Word Saw It		
Eva Peron – Madonna (huh?)		
The Singing Fascist		
	Insert	Cancel

3. Choose what type of item you're referring to in the Reference Type menu. If you're referring to a plain old paragraph, choose Bookmark. Then click outside the dialog box, scroll to the paragraph you're referring to, and place a bookmark there (with the Insert⇨Bookmark command).

4. Your choice in the Insert Reference to box determines whether the reference is to text, a page number, or a numbered item. The options in this box are different, depending on what you chose in Step 3. Roughly, your options are these:

   • **Text:** Choose this option (Heading Text, Bookmark Text, and so on) to include text in the cross-reference. For example, choose Heading Text if your cross-reference is to a heading.

   • **Number:** Choose this option to insert a page number or other kind of number, such as a table number, in the cross-reference.

   • **Above/Below:** Choose this option to enter the word "above" or "below" to tell readers where, in relation to the cross-reference, the thing being referred to is in your document.

5. If you wish, leave the check mark in the Insert as Hyperlink check box to create a hyperlink as well as a cross-reference. (*See* "Hyperlinking in Word 97," earlier in this part, to learn about hyperlinks.)

6. To add the word "above" or "below" to the cross-reference, click the Include Above/Below check box (whether the check box is available depends on which Reference Type option you chose). For example, a cross-reference to a page number would say, "See page 9 below."

7. In the For Which box, tell Word 97 where the thing you're referring to is located. To do so, select a heading, bookmark, footnote, endnote, equation, figure, graph, or whatnot in the menu. In long documents, you will surely have to click the scroll bar to find the one you want.

8. Click Insert.

9. Click the Close button or press Esc.

10. Back in your document, enter the rest of the cross-reference text, if necessary.

When you finish creating your document, update all the cross-references. To do that, press Ctrl and click in the left margin to select the entire document. Then either press F9 or right-click in the document and choose Update Field from the shortcut menu.

TIP

If the thing referred to in a cross-reference is no longer in your document , you see `Error! Reference source not found` where the cross-reference should be. To find cross-reference errors in long documents, look for the word *Error!* with the Edit⇨Find command. Investigate what went wrong and either delete the cross-reference or make a new one.

Putting Footnotes and Endnotes in Documents

COOL STUFF

A *footnote* is a reference, bit of explanation, or comment that appears at the bottom of the page and is referred to by a number or symbol in the text. An *endnote* is the same thing, only it appears at the end of the chapter or document. If you've written a scholarly paper of any kind, you know what a drag footnotes and endnotes are.

Word 97 takes some of the drudgery out of footnotes and endnotes. If you delete or add one, for example, all the others are renumbered. And you don't have to worry about long footnotes because Word 97 adjusts the page layout to make room for them. You can change the numbering scheme of footnotes and endnotes at will.

Inserting a footnote or endnote

To insert a footnote or endnote in a document:

1. Place the cursor in the text where you want the note's symbol or number to appear.

2. Choose Insert⇨Footnote. The Footnote and Endnote dialog box appears.

3. Choose whether you're entering a footnote or endnote in the Insert area of the dialog box.

4. In the Numbering area, click AutoNumber if you want Word 97 to number the notes automatically or Custom Mark to insert a symbol of your own. If you want to insert a symbol, either type it

in the Custom Mark box or click the Symbol button and choose
one from the Symbol dialog box. If you go this route, you have to
enter a symbol each time you insert a note. Not only that, but
you may have to enter two or three symbols for the second and
third notes on each page or document.

5. Click OK. A notes box opens at the bottom of the screen with the
cursor beside the number of the note you're about to enter (if
you don't see this box, switch to Normal View by clicking the
Normal View button in the lower-left corner of the screen or else
choose View➪Normal).

| Footnotes | All Footnotes | ▼ | Close |

¹ Pas en français dans le texte.
² From John Denver, *Rocky Mountain High*; used by kind permission of the songwriter.
3

⁴ Camille Piglia, *Pop Culture in the Fifth Century BC*, 2 vols. (New York: Pitheon, 1992–1994), 2:599. I
have suggested some criticisms of Piglia's treatment of Socrates' guitar playing in a review of her work in
Guitar Player (April, 1996), pp. 45–47.

6. Type your footnote or endnote.

7. Click Close when you're done.

To read a footnote or endnote, carefully put the pointer on top of its
reference number in the text. A yellow box appears with the text of
the footnote or endnote.

Changing the numbering scheme and position of notes

Changing the numbering scheme and positioning of endnotes and
footnotes is quite easy:

1. Choose Insert➪Footnote.

2. Click the Options button in the Footnote and Endnote dialog box.
The Note Options dialog box appears.

Note Options

All Footnotes | All Endnotes

Place at: Bottom of page
Number format: 1, 2, 3, …
Start at: 1
Numbering: ● Continuous
○ Restart each section
○ Restart each page

OK | Cancel | Convert…

3. Click the All Footnotes or All Endnotes tab. The options on these tabs are nearly the same:

- **Place At:** For footnotes, choose Bottom of Page to put footnotes at the bottom of the page no matter where the text ends; choose Beneath Text to put footnotes directly below the last text line on the page. For endnotes, choose End of Section if your document is divided into sections (such as chapters) and you want endnotes to appear at the back of sections; choose End of Document to put all endnotes at the very back of the document.

- **Number Format:** Choose A B C, i ii iii, or another numbering scheme. You can also enter symbols by choosing the last option on this drop-down list.

- **Start At:** To start numbering the notes at a place other than 1, A, or i, enter 2, B, ii, or whatever in this box.

- **Numbering:** To number the notes continuously from the start of your document to the end, choose Continuous. Choose Restart Each Section to begin anew at each section of your document. For footnotes, you can begin anew on each page by choosing Restart Each Page.

- **Convert:** This very convenient button is for fickle scholars who suddenly decide that their endnotes should be footnotes or vice versa. Click it and choose an option in the Convert Notes dialog box to turn footnotes into endnotes, turn endnotes into footnotes, or — in documents with both endnotes and footnotes — make the endnotes footnotes and the footnotes endnotes.

4. Click OK in the Note Options dialog box.

5. Click OK in the Footnote and Endnote dialog box.

Deleting, moving, and editing notes

If a devious editor tells you that a footnote or endnote is in the wrong place, that you don't need a note, or that you need to change the text in a note, all is not lost:

- ✦ **Editing:** To edit a note, select and double-click its number or symbol in the text. The notes box appears at the bottom of the screen. Edit the note at this point.

- ✦ **Moving:** To move a note, select its number or symbol in the text and either drag it to a new location or cut and paste it to a new location.

- ✦ **Deleting:** To delete a note, select its number or symbol and press the Delete key.

Footnotes and endnotes are renumbered when you move or delete them.

Tracking Revisions to Documents

When a lot of hands go into revising a document, figuring out who made revisions to what is impossible. And more importantly, it's impossible to tell what the original, first draft looked like.

To help you keep track of changes to documents, Word 97 offers the Tools⇨Track Changes command. When this command is in effect, all changes to the document are recorded in a different color, with one color for each reviser. New text is underlined, a line is drawn through text that has been deleted, and a vertical line appears in the margin to show where changes were made. By moving the pointer over a change, you can read the name of the person who made it. Then you can accept or reject each change. You can also "compare" the first draft of a document with subsequent drafts to see where changes were made.

To give you an idea of what change marks look like, here are the first two lines of Vladimir Nabokov's autobiography *Speak, Memory* with marks to show where he made changes to his first draft.

> **Vladimir Nabokov, 10/10/96 9:01 PM:**
> Inserted
>
> The cradle rocks above an abyss, and ~~Vulgar~~ common sense ~~Assures~~ tells us that our existence is but a brief ~~strip~~ crack of light between two extremities of ~~complete~~ darkness. Although the two are identical twins, man, as a rule, ~~maybe we~~ views the prenatal abyss ~~one~~ with ~~considerably~~ more calm ~~equanimity~~ than the one he is~~we are~~ heading for (at some forty-five hundred heart beats an hour).

Marking the changes

To keep track of where changes are made to a document, you can either double-click TRK on the status bar, or, if you want to be specific about how changes are recorded, you can do the following:

1. Choose Tools⇨Track Changes⇨Highlight Changes. You see the Highlight Changes dialog box.

2. Click the Track Changes While Editing check box.

3. If you don't want to see the revision marks on-screen, click the Highlight Changes on Screen check box to remove the check mark. Changes to the document are recorded with this option, but they aren't shown. In a document with a lot of revisions, choose this option to work without all that clutter on-screen.

4. Click the Highlight Changes in Printed Document check box if you want change marks to appear on your document when you print it.

5. Click OK.

Now you can start to make changes. If you are the first author to have a crack at this document, your changes appear in blue. If you are the second, they appear in magenta. Word 97 can tell when a new reviser has gotten hold of a document and assigns a new color accordingly.

TIP

To choose a revision color of your own and otherwise tell Word 97 how to mark changes, either choose Tools➪ Track Changes➪ Highlight Changes and click the Options button in the Highlight Changes dialog box, or choose Tools➪Options and click the Track Changes tab in the Options dialog box. Then, with the drop-down lists on the Track Changes tab, tell Word how to mark inserted text, deleted text, changes to formatting, and where to put the line in the margin that shows where changes were made. Be sure to watch the Preview boxes to see what your choices amount to.

Track Changes		? X
Track Changes		
Inserted text	Preview	
Mark: Underline	_ New text _	
Color: By author		
Deleted text	Preview	
Mark: Strikethrough	_ Old text _	
Color: By author		
Changed formatting	Preview	
Mark: Italic	Formatted text	
Color: Black		
Changed lines	Preview	
Mark: Outside border		
Color: Auto		
	OK	Cancel

Comparing and merging documents

 The fastest way to track revisions may be to pass out copies, tell others to make changes, and then "compare" or "merge" the revised document with the original. To compare or merge documents, use the following commands:

✦ **Tools⇨Track Changes⇨Compare Documents:** Choose this command if you are working on a copy of the original document. In the Select File to Compare with Current Document dialog box, find the original file, select it, and choose Open. Marks appear to show where you made changes to the original document.

✦ **Tools⇨Merge Documents:** Choose this command if you have the original document and want to see what others have done to it. In the Select File to Merge Into Current Document dialog box, click the revised version of the file and click Open. Marks show where others made changes to your original document.

Accepting and rejecting revisions

Now that the changes have been made, you can decide what to do about them. Word offers two means of reviewing changes to a document, the Reviewing toolbar and the Accept or Reject Changes dialog box. To review changes one at a time:

1. Choose Tools⇨Track Changes⇨Accept or Reject Changes, or right-click on a toolbar and choose Reviewing from the shortcut menu.

Who made the change

2. To start searching for change marks, click a Find button in the dialog box, or click the Previous Change or Next Change button on the toolbar. Word highlights a change on-screen. In the dialog box, the name of the person who made the revision appears in the Changes box.

3. In the dialog box, click Accept to keep the change, or Reject to reverse it. If you're working with the toolbar, click the Accept Change or Reject Change button.

4. Word finds the next change. Either reject or accept it.

5. To help make sense of what you're doing, you can choose a View option in the dialog box:

- Changes with <u>H</u>ighlighting shows revision marks on-screen.

- Changes <u>w</u>ithout Highlighting shows the changes without the revision marks so you can see what changes will look like if you accept them.

- <u>O</u>riginal shows what the document looked like before any changes were made so you can see what happens to the document if you reject a change.

6. Keep accepting or rejecting. If you change your mind about a revision, click the <u>U</u>ndo button.

7. Click Close or press Esc when you're done.

If you trust your colleagues and have total faith in their revisions, you can accept their revisions in one fell swoop. Click the A<u>c</u>cept All button in the Accept or Reject Changes dialog box. When Word asks whether you really want to accept them all, click <u>Y</u>es. You can reject all the revisions just as easily by choosing Re<u>j</u>ect All.

Potpourri

On the *Jeopardy!* TV show, the last column on the question board is sometimes called "Potpourri." That's where they put oddball questions that can't fit in any category. Part VIII is called "Potpourri," too, because the topics covered here don't fit in the other seven parts of the book.

Some of the tasks in this part are absolutely essential; others are downright wacky. But maybe I'm being "judgmental," as we say in California, and all this stuff is actually very useful. I should let you be the judge of what is and what isn't useful in Part VIII.

In this part . . .

- ✔ Backing up files so that you have copies in case of an emergency
- ✔ Finding a lost file
- ✔ Highlighting important text in a document
- ✔ Importing files from and exporting files to other word processors
- ✔ Protecting your files with passwords

Backing Up Your Work

If an elephant steps on your computer or your computer breaks down and can't be repaired, you lose all the files you worked so hard to create. You have to start from scratch and create your files all over again, unless you backed them up. *Backing up* means to make a copy of a file and put it on a floppy disk, tape drive, or other place from which you can retrieve files in the event of a fire, pestilence, coffee spill, computer breakdown, or other emergency.

Besides backing up files to a floppy disk or tape drive, you can back up files in special directories on your hard disk. The disadvantage of backing up this way, however, is that the files are still on your computer. If your computer breaks down altogether, you can't get your files back. However, you can recover them if there is a power failure or other untoward event that doesn't damage your computer.

Backing up to a floppy disk or tape drive

To back up a file to a location outside your computer, you leave Word 97 and do the job with Windows 95:

1. Close the file if it is open.

2. Open the Explorer utility in Windows 95. To do this, click the Start button, choose Programs, and choose Windows Explorer from the Programs list. The Windows Explorer window appears on-screen.

3. Find the file you want to back up. To get to my Word 97 files, I click the plus sign next to MSOffice in the All Folders pane on the left side of the Explorer window. Then I click the plus sign next to Winword to see my Winword folders. Then I click the folder with the file I want to back up. When I click the folder, the files in the folder appear in the Contents Of window pane on the right side of the screen.

4. When you see the file you're backing up, click and drag it to the place where you will store the backup copy. To store it on a floppy disk, for example, drag it to the Floppy icon at the top of the All Folders window pane and release the mouse button.

The Copying message box appears. It tells you that the file is being copied and shows a picture of pieces of paper being flung from one folder to another.

Now you can get the file back by copying it from the floppy disk or tape drive to your computer. Be sure to save your floppy disk or backup tape in a safe place away from your computer. A fire, for example, would destroy your computer and your backup files if you keep your backups on the desk next to your computer.

Backing up files in Word 97

You can recover files that have been backed up or saved automatically if you accidentally unplug the computer, a power failure occurs, or your computer hangs. To tell Word 97 to back up and save files automatically:

1. Choose Tools⇨Options.

2. Click the Save tab of the Options dialog box.

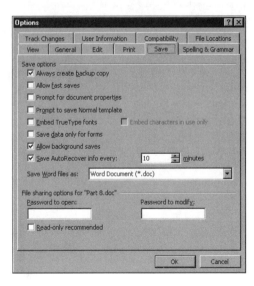

3. Click the Always Create Backup Copy check box.

4. Click the Save AutoRecover Info Every check box and enter a number in the Minutes box to tell Word 97 how often to make a document recovery file. Word uses these files to restore documents that were on the screen when the computer died.

5. Click OK.

After you choose the Always Create Backup Copy and Save AutoRecover Info Every options, you can get copies of files after a power failure. So why would you choose one option over the other, or both options? Here's why:

✦ **Save AutoRecover Info Every:** With this option, Word 97 makes a document recovery copy of your file every few minutes (depending on what you enter in the Minutes box). After a power failure occurs and you start Word again, the application opens the AutoRecover files of the documents that were on-screen when the computer died. These documents aren't entirely up to date, but they are good as of the last time Word made the document recovery file.

✦ **Always Create Backup Copy:** With this option, Word makes a second copy of your file and keeps it in the same folder as the original. However, the backup copy is made only when you, and not Word 97, save the file. If a power failure occurs, you can't recover the work you did in the last few minutes, although you can recover the version of the file that was saved the last time *you* saved the file.

Backup copies made with the Always Create Backup Copy option eat up a lot of disk space. If you choose this option, two copies of everything you do in Word 97 are stored on disk. That takes up a lot of room.

Recovering a file with AutoRecover

Suppose a power failure occurs. To recover a file from its AutoRecover cousin:

1. Start Word 97. All the documents that you were working on when lightning struck are opened on-screen. You see (*rec*) after their names.

2. Choose File⇨Save As.

3. Click the Save button in the Save As dialog box.

4. Click Yes when Word 97 asks whether you want to replace the existing document.

The work you did in the last few minutes is lost, but the work that was complete last time Word 97 made an AutoRecover copy of the file is restored.

Opening a backup copy of a file

To get the backup copy of a file after a power failure or other electrical accident:

1. Click the Open button, press Ctrl+O, or choose File⇨Open to display the Open dialog box.

2. Go to the folder where the original file was stored and click on it.

3. Click the down arrow on the Files of Type box at the bottom of the dialog box and choose All Files.

4. Look for the backup copy and click on it. Backup copy names start with the words *Backup of* and end with the *.wbk* extension.

5. Click Open.

Finding a Missing File

Occasionally, you forget the name of a file you want to open. Or you remember the name but forget the name of the folder you put the file in. When that happens, you can search for the file with options in the Open dialog box:

1. Click the Open button, press Ctrl+O, or choose File⇨Open to get to the Open dialog box.

2. Choose options at the bottom of the dialog box:

- **File Name:** Enter the filename if you know it. If you vaguely remember the name, you can use wildcards to help with the search (*see* "Searching with Wildcards in Part V to learn how to use wildcards). If you're utterly confused, don't worry. You can leave this box blank.

- **Files of Type:** Click the down arrow and choose the type of file you're looking for. Most likely, it is Word Documents, but you can choose All Files or another option.

- **Text or Property:** If you can remember a word or phrase from the document you're looking for, enter it here in quotation marks. For example, type **"Dear Mom"** if you're searching for a letter to your mother.

- **Last Modified:** Click the down arrow and choose an option that best describes when you last saved the file.

3. Click the Find Now button. The file or files that match the criteria you just entered appear in the Open dialog box.

4. Click a file and choose Open to open it.

If Word 97 can't find a file that matches your criteria, `0 files(s) found` appears in the lower-left corner of the Open dialog box. Change the criteria by clicking the New Search button and starting all over again.

Getting Information about a Document

 Word 97 keeps information about your documents. You can find out how long you've worked on a document, how many times you've saved it, when you created it, and how many words it contains, among other things. You can also enter words to help Word 97 find your document if it is lost.

 The fast way to get the statistics on a document is to choose Tools⇨Word Count. A dialog box appears with the number of words, characters, pages, and lines.

To get detailed stats on a document:

1. Choose File⇨Properties.

2. Click the tabs to review or make changes on them.

3. Click OK.

The Statistics tab tells when the document was created, when and who last saved it, and how much work went into it in terms of time, pages, words, and characters, among other things.

Part 8.doc Properties

General | Summary | Statistics | Contents | Custom

Created: Friday, September 22, 1995 11:36:00 AM
Modified: Thursday, October 03, 1996 10:06:10 AM
Accessed: Thursday, October 03, 1996
Printed:

Last saved by: Peter Weverka
Revision number: 41
Total editing time: 155 Minutes

Statistics:

Statistic name	Value
Pages:	12
Paragraphs:	202
Lines:	378
Words:	3893
Characters:	17480
Characters (with spaces):	21069
Bytes:	47616

OK | Cancel

The Summary tab lists the author, title, and other pertinent information. If you think that you might lose your file someday, enter words in the Category and Keywords boxes to help Windows 95 find the file. Click the Save Preview Picture box to put a picture of the first page of the document in the Open dialog box instead of the standard Word 97 document icon.

The General tab tells you how long the file is and whether it's an archive, read-only, hidden, or system file.

The Contents tab tells you which subdocuments are in the file, if your file is a master document.

The Custom tab lets you create other means of keeping statistics on your documents.

Highlighting Parts of a Document

One way to call attention to the most important parts of a document is to highlight them. You can do that very easily with the Highlight button on the Formatting toolbar:

1. Scroll to the part of the document you want to highlight.

2. Click on the highlight button. The cursor changes into a fat pencil.

3. Drag the cursor over the text you want to highlight.

4. Click the Highlight button again when you're done.

To choose a color for highlighting, click the down arrow beside the Highlight button and then click a color on the color menu.

Highlight marks are printed along with the text. To get rid of them, follow these steps:

1. Select the document or the text from which you want to remove the highlights.

2. Click the down arrow to open the Highlight color menu.

3. Click None.

Importing and Exporting Files

Word 97 makes it easy to use files from other Microsoft Office applications, from other versions of Microsoft Word (including Macintosh versions), from Write and Works, and from WordPerfect. Other files are a different story. For example, Word 97 is not on speaking terms with WordPro, not to mention antique word processors like WordStar and XYWrite.

It is easy to export files to and import files from applications that Word recognizes and is friendly with. Your coworkers who have WordPerfect, for example, can use your files, but your friends who have other word processors may well have to use stripped-down versions of your files with the text but none of the formats.

Even when you import or export a file successfully, some things get lost. For example, special characters and symbols often don't translate well. Nor do certain fonts. Proofread files that you've imported or exported carefully to make sure that everything came out right.

Importing a file

To import a file, you open it and let Word 97 turn it into a Word 97 file:

1. Click the Open button, press Ctrl+O, or choose File⇨Open to display the Open dialog box.

2. Find the file you want to import in the Open dialog box and click it.

3. Click the down arrow in the Files of Type box and see whether the kind of file you want to import is on the list. If it is, click it. If it isn't, try choosing Rich Text Format. This format strives to retain all the formatting of non-Word documents. If worse comes to worse, you can always click the Text Files option. With this option, Word strips all formats such as boldfacing and fonts from the file, but at least you get to keep the text.

4. Click Open.

Here's one way to get around file-importing impasses: If the application you want to import the file from works in Windows 95, open the application, open the file you want to copy, and copy the parts of the file you need to the Clipboard. Then paste what is on the Clipboard into Word 97.

Another way to get around the problem of not being able to import a file is to see whether the other application can save files in Microsoft Word format. If it can, save the file as a Microsoft Word file in the other application and then open it in Word 97.

Word 97 files cannot be viewed or worked on in Word 97's predecessor, Word 95 (also known as Word 7). To pass along a file to a friend or coworker who has Word 95, save the file as a Word 95 file. Read on to find out how.

Exporting a file

To export a file so that someone with another kind of word processor can use it, you save the file in a new format:

1. Choose File⇨Save As.

2. Find the file you want to export in the Save As dialog box and click it.

3. Click the down arrow in the Save as Type menu and see whether the kind of file you want to export is on the list. If it is on the list, choose it. If it isn't, choose either Rich Text Format or Text Only with Line Breaks:

- Rich Text Format retains the formatting of the text, but some word processors can't understand it.

- In case worse comes to worse, Text Only with Line Breaks strips out all the formatting but retains the text and line breaks.

4. Click Save.

Including Video Clips, Animation, and Sound in Documents

The bigwig visionaries of the computer industry have for years been predicting that someday soon all documents will include sound and animation sequences. Video and sound are way, way too complex for this book. But if you want to bravely go where few nerds have gone before and include sound or video in a document, this entry outlines the basic steps.

To "animate" words in a document, select them, choose Format⇨Font, click the Animation tab in the Font dialog box, make a choice from the Animations list (the Preview box shows precisely what you are choosing), and click OK. The (none) option in the Animations list is for removing text animations.

For more-sophisticated multimedia, follow these steps:

1. Place the cursor where you want the sound or animation to go.

2. Choose Insert⇨Object. The Object dialog box appears.

3. What you do next depends on whether the object exists yet:

- **Create New tab:** On the Create New tab box, choose what you want to insert. The Result box at the bottom of the dialog box describes the different objects you can insert. Click OK. Depending on what you choose, Word 97 opens either another application or a special window for creating the sound byte or video sequence.

- **Create from File tab:** Click the Create from File tab and locate the file whose sound, animation sequence, or video clip you want to put in your document.

You're on your own, and may the force be with you.

Protecting Your Work with Passwords

To keep jealous coworkers, your spouse, your boss, and unauthorized biographers from opening a file, you can protect it with a password. You can also allow others to view a document but not make changes to it unless they have the password. You can even protect a part of a document to keep others from changing it.

Keeping others from opening a file

To keep others from opening a document unless they have the password:

1. Open the document.

2. Choose Tools⇨Options and click the Save tab in the Options dialog box.

3. Type your password in the Password to Open box. Instead of letters, asterisks appear in the box in case a spy is looking over your shoulder (that spy, however, could watch your fingers to see which letters you type). Passwords can be 15 characters long. If you include upper- and lowercase letters in your password, remember them well because you have to reproduce your password exactly whenever you open this file.

4. Click OK.

5. In the Confirm Password dialog box, type the password again. If you don't enter it correctly, Word 97 tells you so and sends you back to the Options dialog box.

6. Click OK in the Confirm Password dialog box.

After you attach a password to a document, you have to save the document to make the password go into effect.

It almost goes without saying, but you must never, never forget your password. If you forget it, you simply cannot open the file again!

Everybody has different advice for choosing a password that isn't likely to be forgotten or discovered, and everybody agrees that you shouldn't use your name or the names of family members or pets, because miscreants try those names first when they try to crack open a file. Here's a good tip for choosing passwords: Pick your favorite foreign city and spell it backwards. My favorite foreign city is in Chile. If I needed a password, it would be **ogaitnaS**.

Opening a password-protected file

To open a file that has been given a password:

1. Open the file as you normally would. The Password dialog box appears.

2. Type the password and click OK.

If Word 97 tells you that it can't open the file because you've given the wrong password, you may have entered the password with the wrong combination of upper- and lowercase characters. Try again using different capital letters and lowercase letters.

Removing a password

To remove a password, all you have to do is this:

1. Open the file.

2. Choose Tools➪Options.

3. Click the Save tab.

4. Delete the asterisks from the Password to Open box.

5. Click OK.

Keeping others from changing a file

Besides keeping others from looking at a file, you can keep them from making changes to a file unless they have the password. This way, others can open the file, but they must have the password in order to edit it.

1. Open the document.

2. Choose Tools➪Options and click the Save tab in the Options dialog box.

3. Type your password in the Password to Modify box. The usual asterisks appear as you type the password.

4. Click OK.

5. In the Confirm Password dialog box, type the password again.

6. Click OK.

Whenever anyone tries to open this file, he or she sees this dialog box:

By entering the correct password and clicking OK, the other user can view and make changes to the file. If the other user doesn't have the password, he or she can still view and make changes to the file by clicking the Read Only button. However, when the other user tries to save the file, he or she will have to save it, along with the changes made to it, under a different filename.

Protecting parts of a document from changes

With Word 97's Tools⇨Protect Document command, you can prevent others from making changes in various ways. You can keep users who don't have the password from changing annotations and forms, and you can also force all changes made to the document to be recorded with revision marks. Here's how:

1. Open the document you want to protect.

2. Choose Tools⇨Protect Document. The Protect Document dialog box appears:

3. In the Protect document for area, choose how you want to protect the file:

- **Tracked Changes:** All changes made to the document are recorded with revision marks. This way, you always know where changes were made.

- **Comments:** Reviewers can make their own comments but can't change the comments that are there already.

- **Forms:** Users can fill in form fields, but they can't change the text of the form.

4. If you want to protect the forms in only one or two sections in a document, make sure that the Forms option button is selected, click the Sections button, and click to remove the check marks from the sections you *don't* want to protect. Then click OK.

5. Enter a password in the Password box. Passwords can be 15 characters long. Remember this password and the exact combination of upper- and lowercase letters because you and other users need to type it the same way when you want to make changes to comments or forms or make changes without the revision marks showing.

6. Click OK to close the Protect Document dialog box.

Now users have to enter the correct password to change existing comments or forms or track changes without revision marks.

To "unprotect" a document so that users can make changes at will, choose Tools⇨Unprotect document.

Techie Talk

AutoCorrect: Word 97 "autocorrects" what it thinks are errors in documents. Certain words are autocorrected, as are capitalization errors.

cell: The box that is formed in a table where a row and column intersect. Each cell holds one data item.

check box: A square box inside a dialog box. Click an option's check box to place a check mark in the box and activate the option. Click again to remove the check mark and render the option dormant.

click: To press the left mouse button once. Not to be confused with *clique,* a like-minded assortment of high school students who dress and talk the same way. *See also* right-click.

clip art: Graphics and pictures that can be imported into a computer file.

Clipboard: A holding tank to which you can copy or move text and graphics. Text and graphics can be pasted from the Clipboard into a document.

crop: To cut off part of a graphic.

curb feeler: A flexible metal rod that was attached to the right rear bumper of most pre-1955 cars. Curb feelers helped with parallel parking, as drivers heard a scraping noise when their cars came too close to the curb.

cursor: An on-screen symbol that tells you what the computer is doing. Cursors include the insertion point, the vertical line that blinks on and off and tells you where text goes when you press the keys, and the mouse cursor, which looks like an arrow when you move the mouse over something you can choose or like a large egotistical *I* when it is in a document window. Also someone who curses at a computer screen.

dialog box: A box that appears on-screen when Word 97 needs more information to complete a task. Fill in the dialog box and click the OK button to give a command. *See also* check box, drop-down list, option button, radio button.

document: A letter, report, announcement, or proclamation that you create with Word. Any file you create with Word 97 is considered a document.

double-click: To click twice with the left mouse button.

drag and drop: The fastest way to copy or move text from one place to another. Select the text, hold down the left mouse button, drag the text to a new location, and release the mouse button.

drop-down list: A menu box with a down arrow at its side. Click the down arrow, and a menu appears with options you can choose.

field: A code in a file that represents information that varies. For example, if you put a "today's date" field at the top of a letter you write on July 31, 1997, but print the letter on August 5, 1997, the letter is dated August 5, 1997. Also a flat place where soccer is played or crops are grown.

file extension: The three-character extension following the period in filenames. Word 97 files have the *.doc* (document) extension. Each type of computer file has its own three-letter file extension.

font: A typeface design.

footer: A line at the bottom of each page of a document with the document's name, a page number, or similar information. *See also* header.

function keys: The ten or twelve F keys along the top of the key-board. Function keys are used to give commands.

gutter: In a bound document, the part of the paper that the binding eats into. Also, in a newspaper-style document, the space between columns.

header: A line at the top of the pages of a document that lists the document's name, the page number, or similar information. *See also* footer.

header row: The labels along the top row or rows of a table or database that explain what is in the columns below.

hot key: The underlined letter in a command name. Press the hot key or Alt + the hot key to execute a command quickly.

hyperlink: A link between two documents or two different places in the same document. By clicking the hyperlink, you go directly to the other document or other place in the same document.

kerning: To make a pair of letters farther apart or closer together.

leading: The vertical distance between two lines of type.

margin: The empty space on a page between the text and the top, bottom, left, and right borders of the page. Text is indented from the margin, not the side of the page.

mouse: The soap-shaped thing on your desk that you roll to make the mouse cursor move on-screen. If you reach for your mouse and feel fur or hear a squeaking sound, you should stop eating at your desk. The mouse has a left and right button. *See also* click, cursor, right-click.

object: A catchall term for something that can be put in a Word 97 document that isn't related to text — for example, sound bytes and graphics.

option button: A button in a dialog box that you click to perform a task or open another dialog box.

orphan: A single line of text at the start of a paragraph that appears at the very bottom of a page. Orphans sort of cheat the reader, because the reader can't tell how long the paragraph is until he or she turns the page. *See also* widow.

paste: To copy text or a graphic from the Clipboard to a document.

point: A unit for measuring type size. One point equals $1/72$ of an inch.

radio button: One of a set of two or more option buttons, only one of which can be selected. Radio buttons are round.

right-click: To click with the right mouse button.

save: To copy the data on-screen to the computer's hard disk. Data is not stored permanently until it has been saved.

scroll: To move through a document or menu by using the scroll bars along the right side or, in the case of wide documents, using the scroll bar at the bottom of the screen as well.

section: A part of a document. You cannot change page numbering schemes or margin sizes without creating a new section.

shortcut menu: A menu that appears when you right-click on-screen. Which shortcut menu appears depends on which part of the screen you click.

sort: To arrange the data in a table in a new way.

style: A format for headings, paragraphs, and other parts of a document, as well as characters. You can assign a new style by choosing one from the Style menu on the Formatting toolbar. Never to be confused with the term as it is used to describe a unique way of dressing.

taskbar: The bar along the bottom of the screen in Windows 95. The names of computer applications that are running appear on buttons on the taskbar. Click a button to switch to another application.

template: A collection of styles you can choose from for formatting documents. All the styles in a template appear in the Style menu on the Formatting toolbar. *See also* style.

toolbar: An assortment of buttons for performing tasks.

typeface: *See* font.

typewriter: A device used by the ancient Egyptians for imprinting letters on papyrus leaves. According to some archeologists, the typewriter is the forerunner of the word processor.

widow: A very short line, usually one word, that appears at the end of a paragraph. Widows create a lot of ugly white space across the page. *See also* orphan.

Index

T